PLOTINUS
ENNEAD IV.8

THE *ENNEADS* OF PLOTINUS
WITH PHILOSOPHICAL COMMENTARIES

Series editors: John M. Dillon, Trinity College, Dublin and Andrew Smith, University College Dublin

TITLES FORTHCOMING IN THE SERIES INCLUDE:

Ennead I.6:
On the Beautiful
by Andrew Smith

Ennead IV.3–IV.5:
On Problems of the Soul I, II, & III
by John M. Dillon and Gary Gurtler

Ennead IV.7:
On the Immortality of the Soul
by Barrie Fleet

Ennead V.5:
That the Intelligibles are not Outside the Intellect, and on the Good
by Lloyd Gerson

Ennead V.8:
On Intelligible Beauty
by Andrew Smith

Ennead VI.4 & VI.5:
On the Presence of Being, One and the Same, Everywhere as a Whole I & II
by Eyjólfur Emilsson

Ennead VI.8:
On Free Will and the Will of the One
by Kevin Corrigan

PLOTINUS
ENNEAD IV.8

On the Descent of the Soul into Bodies

Translation with an Introduction and Commentary

BARRIE FLEET

PARMENIDES
PUBLISHING
Las Vegas | Zurich | Athens

PARMENIDES PUBLISHING
Las Vegas | Zurich | Athens

This edition published in 2012 by Parmenides Publishing
in the United States of America

ISBN soft cover: 978-1-930972-77-3
ISBN e-Book: 978-1-930972-78-0

Library of Congress Cataloging-in-Publication Data

Plotinus.
[Enneads. IV, 8. English]
Ennead IV.8 : on the descent of the soul into bodies / Plotinus ;
translation with an introduction and commentary by Barrie Fleet.
p. cm. — (The enneads of Plotinus with philosophical
commentaries)
Includes bibliographical references (p.) and indexes.
ISBN 978-1-930972-77-3 (pbk. : alk. paper) —
ISBN 978-1-930972-78-0 (e-book)
1. Mind and body—Early works to 1800. 2. Soul—Early works to
1800. 3. Plotinus. Enneads. 4. Neoplatonism. I. Fleet, Barrie. II.
Title. III. Title: On the descent of the soul into bodies.
B693.E52E5 2012
186'.4—dc23

2012009748

Typeset in Janson Text and Frutiger
by 1106 Design | www.1106design.com
Printed digitally by Edwards Brothers, Chicago, IL

1-888-PARMENIDES
www.parmenides.com

Contents

Introduction to the Series With a Brief Outline of the Life and Thought of Plotinus (205–270 CE)

PLOTINUS WAS BORN IN 205 CE in Egypt of Greek-speaking parents. He attended the philosophical schools in Alexandria where he would have studied Plato (427–347 BCE), Aristotle (384–322 BCE), the Stoics and Epicureans as well as other Greek philosophical traditions. He began his serious philosophical education, however, relatively late in life, at the age of twenty-seven and was deeply impressed by the Platonist Ammonius Saccas about whom we, unfortunately, know very little, but with whom Plotinus studied for some eleven years. Even our knowledge of Plotinus' life is limited to what we can glean from Porphyry's introduction to his edition of his philosophical treatises, an account colored by Porphyry's own concerns. After completing his studies in Alexandria Plotinus attempted, by joining a military expedition of the Roman emperor Gordian III, to make contact with the Brahmins in order to learn something of Indian thought. Unfortunately Gordian was defeated and killed (244). Plotinus somehow managed to extract himself and we next hear of him in Rome where he was able to set up a school of philosophy in the house of a high-ranking Roman lady by the name of Gemina. It is, perhaps, surprising that he had no formal contacts with the Platonic Academy in Athens, which was headed at the time by Longinus, but Longinus was familiar with his work, partly at least through Porphyry who had studied in Athens. The fact that it was Rome where Plotinus set up his school may be due to the originality of his philosophical activity and to his patrons. He clearly had some influential contacts, not least with the philhellenic emperor Gallienus (253–268), who may also have encouraged his later failed attempt to set up a civic community based on Platonic principles in a ruined city in Campania.

Plotinus' school was, like most ancient schools of philosophy, relatively small in scale, but did attract distinguished students from abroad and from the Roman upper classes. It included not only philosophers but politicians and members of the medical profession who wished to lead the philosophical life. His most famous student was Porphyry (233–305 CE) who as a relative latecomer to the school persuaded him to put into writing the results of his seminars. It is almost certain that we possess most, if not all, of his written output, which represents his mature thought, since he didn't commence writing until the age of forty-eight. The school seemingly had inner and outer circles, and Plotinus himself was clearly an inspiring and sympathetic teacher who took a deep interest in the philosophical and spiritual progress of his students. Porphyry tells us that when he was suffering from severe depression Plotinus straight away visited him in his lodgings to help him. His concern for others is also illustrated by the fact that he was entrusted with the personal education of many orphans and the care of their property and careers. The reconciliation of this worldly involvement with the encouragement to lead a life of contemplation is encapsulated in Porphyry's comment that "he was present to himself and others at the same time."

The *Enneads* of Plotinus is the edition of his treatises arranged by his pupil Porphyry who tried to put shape to the collection he had inherited by organizing it into six sets of nine treatises (hence the name "*Enneads*") that led the reader through the levels of Plotinus' universe, from the physical world to Soul, Intellect and, finally, to the highest principle, the One. Although Plotinus undoubtedly had a clearly structured metaphysical system by the time he began committing himself to expressing his thought in written form, the treatises themselves are not systematic expositions, but rather explorations of particular themes and issues raised in interpreting Plato and other philosophical texts read in the School.

In fact, to achieve his neat arrangement Porphyry was sometimes driven even to dividing certain treatises (e.g., II.2–3; IV.3–5 and VI.4–5).

Although Plotinus' writings are not transcripts of his seminars, but are directed to the reader, they do, nevertheless, convey the sort of lively debate that he encouraged in his school. Frequently he takes for granted that a particular set of ideas is already familiar as having been treated in an earlier seminar that may or may not be found in the written text. For this reason it is useful for the reader to have some idea of the main philosophical principles of his system as they can be extracted from the *Enneads* as a whole.

Plotinus regarded himself as a faithful interpreter of Plato whose thought lies at the core of his entire project. But Plato's thought, whilst definitive, does according to Plotinus require careful exposition and clarification, often in the light of other thinkers such as Aristotle and the Stoics. It is because of this creative application of different traditions of ancient thought to the interpretation of Plato that Plotinus' version of Platonism became, partly through the medium of later Platonists such as Porphyry, Iamblichus (245–325) and Proclus (412–485), an influential source and way of reading both Plato and Aristotle in the Middle Ages, the Renaissance, and up to the early 19th century, when scholars first began to differentiate Plato and "Neoplatonism." His thought, too, provided early Christian theologians of the Latin and particularly of the Byzantine tradition, with a rich variety of metaphysical concepts with which to explore and express difficult doctrinal ideas. His fashioning of Plato's ideas into a consistent metaphysical structure, though no longer accepted as a uniquely valid way of approaching Plato, was influential in promoting the notion of metaphysical systems in early modern philosophy. More recently increasing interest has centered on his exploration of the self, levels of consciousness, and his expansion of discourse beyond the levels of normal ontology to the examination of what lies both above and beneath being. His thought continues to challenge us when confronted with the issue of man's nature and role in the universe and of the extent and limitations of human knowledge.

Whilst much of Plotinus' metaphysical structure is recognizably an interpretation of Plato it is an interpretation that is not always immediately obvious just because it is filtered through several centuries of developing Platonic thought, itself already overlaid with important concepts drawn from other schools. It is, nevertheless, useful as a starting point to see how Plotinus attempts to bring coherence to what he believed to be a comprehensive worldview expressed in the Platonic dialogues. The Platonic Forms are central. They become for him an intelligible universe that is the source and model of the physical universe. But aware of Aristotle's criticism of the Platonic Forms as lifeless causes he takes on board

Aristotle's concept of god as a self-thinker to enable him to identify this intelligible universe as a divine Intellect that thinks itself as the Forms or Intelligibles. The doctrine of the Forms as the thoughts of God had already entered Platonism, but not as the rigorously argued identity that Plotinus proposed. Moreover the Intelligibles, since they are identical with Intellect, are themselves actively intellectual; they are intellects. Thus Plato's world of Forms has become a complex and dynamic intelligible universe in which unity and plurality, stability and activity are reconciled.

Now although the divine Intellect is one it also embraces plurality both because its thoughts, the Intelligibles, are many and because it may itself be analyzed into thinker and thought. Its unity demands a further principle which is the cause of its unity. This principle which is the cause of all unity and being, but does not possess unity or being in itself, he calls the One, an interpretation of the Idea of the Good in Plato's *Republic* that is "beyond being" and that may be seen as the simple (hence "one") source of all reality. We thus have the first two of what subsequently became known as the three Hypostases, the One, Intellect, and Soul, the last of which acts as an intermediary between the intelligible and physical universes. This last Hypostasis takes on all the functions of transmitting form and life that may be found in Plato, although Plato himself does not always make such a clear distinction between soul and intellect. Thus the One is the ultimate source of all, including this universe, which is then prefigured in Intellect and transmitted through Soul to become manifest as our physical universe. Matter, which receives imperfectly this expression, is conceived not as an independently existing counter-principle, a dangerously dualist notion, but is in a sense itself a product of the One, a kind of non-being that, while being nothing specific in itself, nevertheless is not simply not there.

But this procession from an ultimate principle is balanced by a return movement at each level of reality that fully constitutes itself only when it turns back in contemplation of its producer. And so the whole of reality is a dynamic movement of procession and return, except for matter, which has no life of its own to make this return; it is inert. This movement of return, which may be traced back to the force of "love" in Plato or Aristotle's final cause, is characterized by Plotinus as a cognitive activity, a form of contemplation, weaker at each successive level, from Intellect through discursive reasoning to the merest image of rational order as expressed in the objects of the physical universe.

The human individual mirrors this structure to which we are all related at each level. For each of us has a body and soul, an intellect, and even something within us that relates to the One. While it is the nature of soul to give life to body, the higher aspect of our soul also has aspirations towards intellect, the true self, and even beyond. This urge to return corresponds to the cosmic movement of return. But the tension between soul's natural duty to body and its origins in the intelligible can be, for the individual, a source of fracture and alienation in which the soul becomes over-involved and overwhelmed by the body and so estranged from its true self. Plotinus encourages us to make the return or ascent, but at the same time attempts to resolve the conflict of duties by reconciling the two-fold nature of soul as life-giving and contemplative.

This is the general framework within which important traditional philosophical issues are encountered, discussed and resolved, but always in a spirit of inquiry and ongoing debate. Issues are frequently encountered in several different contexts, each angle providing a different insight. The nature of the soul and its relationship to the body is examined at length (IV) using the Aristotelian distinctions of levels of soul (vegetative, growth, sensitive, rational) whilst maintaining the immortal nature of the transcendent soul in Platonic terms. The active nature of the soul in sense-perception is maintained to preserve the principle that incorporeals cannot be affected by corporeal reality. A vigorous discussion (VI.4 and 5) on the general nature of the relationship of incorporeals to body explores in every detail and in great depth the way in which incorporeals act on body. A universe that is the product of design is reconciled with the freedom of the individual. And, not least, the time-bound nature of the physical universe and human reason is grounded in the life of Intellect which subsists in eternity. Sometimes, however, Plotinus seems to break outside the framework of traditional metaphysics: the nature of matter and the One, each as non-being, though in a different sense, strains the terminology and structure of traditional ontology; and the attempt to reconcile the role of the individual soul within the traditional Platonic distinction of transcendent and immanent reality leads to a novel exploration of the nature of the self, the "I."

It is this restless urge for exploration and inquiry that lends to the treatises of Plotinus their philosophical vitality. Whilst presenting us with a rich and complexly coherent system, he constantly engages us in philosophical inquiry. In this way each treatise presents us with new ideas and fresh challenges. And, for Plotinus, every philosophical engagement is not just a mental exercise but also contributes to the rediscovery of the self and our reintegration with the source of all being, the Platonic aim of "becoming like god."

While Plotinus, like Plato, always wishes to engage his audience to reflect for themselves, his treatises are not easy reading, partly no doubt because his own audience was already familiar with many of his basic ideas and, more importantly, had been exposed in his seminars to critical readings of philosophical texts that have not survived to our day. Another problem is that the treatises do not lay out his thought in a systematic way but take up specific issues, although always the whole system may be discerned in the background. Sometimes, too, the exact flow of thought is difficult to follow because of an often condensed mode of expression. Because we are convinced that Plotinus has something to say to us today we have launched this series of translations and commentaries as a means of opening up the text to readers with an interest in grappling with the philosophical issues revealed by an encounter with Plotinus' own words and arguments. Each volume will contain a new translation, careful summaries of the arguments and structure of the treatise, and a philosophical commentary that will aim to throw light on the philosophical meaning and import of the text.

John M. Dillon
Andrew Smith

Abbreviations

HS_1	*Plotini Opera*, edited by P. Henry and H.-R. Schwyzer, vol. 1. Paris & Brussels, 1959 (edition major).
HS_2	*Plotini Opera*, edited by P. Henry and H.-R. Schwyzer, vol. 2. Oxford: 1977 (edition minor) = OCT.
KRS	*The Presocratic Philosophers*, edited by G. Kirk, J. Raven, and M. Schofield, 2nd ed. Cambridge, UK: 1983.
Loeb	*Plotinus*, edited by A. H. Armstrong, 7 vols. Cambridge, MA & London: 1966–1988.
LS	*The Hellenistic Philosophers*, A. A. Long and D. Sedley. Cambridge: 1987.
MacK	*Plotinus. The Enneads*, translated by S. MacKenna, 2nd ed. London: 1930.
OCT	Oxford Classical Text.
SVF	*Stoicorum Veterum Fragmenta*, edited by H. von Arnim. Leipzig: 1905–1924.
VP	*Vita Plotini* = Porphyry's Life of Plotinus printed at start of HS_1, HS_2, MacK and Loeb.

Acknowledgments

THE AUTHOR WISHES TO EXPRESS his gratitude to John Dillon and Andrew Smith for their valuable advice on the substance of the introduction, translation and commentary, and to Eliza Tutellier and the editorial team at Parmenides Press for their excellent work on producing the final version of the book.

Introduction to the Treatise

PLOTINUS WAS FIRST AND FOREMOST a Platonist, committed to expounding the doctrines of Plato in the light of the philosophical activity of the intervening seven centuries. In Plato's works there are difficulties and inconsistencies, and this is recognized on several occasions by Plotinus, as in the first chapter of this treatise: "It is clear that he (Plato) does not always speak with sufficient consistency for us to make out his intentions with any ease" (lines 27–28). This treatise, IV.8 [6], shows Plotinus grappling with one such question: how is it that the soul descends into the body? This leads to further questions about the nature of soul and of the cosmos at large. In the background are other unresolved issues in Plato, such as the contrast between the optimistic view of the sensible world found in *Timaeus* and the more pessimistic picture painted elsewhere, notably in *Phaedo*. Further, as the treatise unfolds, the apparently conflicting roles of necessity and of free choice come more to the fore.[1]

Porphyry in his *Life of Plotinus* (*Vita Plotini* = *VP* 14) tells us that Plotinus held seminars *(sunousiai)* where works of followers of Plato, such as Numenius, and of Aristotle, such as Alexander, were read and discussed; no doubt the writings of both Plato and Aristotle were to hand, although, to judge by his occasional misquotations, Plotinus was perhaps sometimes working from memory. Works of Plato germane to this treatise are *Republic*, *Symposium*, *Phaedrus*, *Phaedo*, *Theaetetus*, *Timaeus* and *Letter* 7. Key to *our* interpretation of Plotinus' text is an understanding of *his* interpretation of Plato's texts, which will figure large in the commentary. Plotinus wrote down the findings of these seminars, but since he was impatient, poorly sighted and possibly dyslexic (*VP* 8), they needed careful editing, a task which Porphyry took on himself. He put the main treatises concerning the soul together as *Ennead* IV, which includes this short treatise. Although Porphyry himself gives in some cases different titles to the same treatise in his *Life of Plotinus*, the title of this treatise, "On the descent of soul into bodies" is the same in both of his tables, and echoes Plato's phrase at *Republic* 517b5 "the ascent of the soul into the intelligible region."

Porphyry (*VP* 4) tells us that this treatise was chronologically the sixth, written by Plotinus some

[1] See further Henry (1938, ch. 1) and Dufour (2003, 117–124).

years before Porphyry joined his circle in 263 CE. In what follows, when referring to other treatises, I have added the chronological number only where it affects the argument.

By way of introduction let us briefly consider three questions, both in the light of Plato's teachings and of Plotinus' perception of those teachings. First, what is the nature of soul? Secondly, what is the nature of the soul's ascent? Thirdly, what does the soul achieve at the end of its ascent?

The Nature of Soul

For Plato, soul—as described in *Timaeus*—is broadly divided into two categories. First, there is the soul of the cosmos, sometimes known as the world soul. At *Timaeus* 34b–36d he describes at some length the complexities of the creation of the soul of the cosmos by the divine craftsman. (It is unclear whether he thought that the divine craftsman had a separate soul.) For us the significant points are that it is "prior to body in both excellence and generation" (34c4), that it is spread throughout the created cosmos and was even "wrapped around it from outside" (34b3 & 36el), and that it has cognizance of both the intelligible and of the sensible world, which it directs and organises (37ab).[2] Secondly, there are individual souls

[2] See further Guthrie (1978, vol. 5, 292–299), and Cornford (1937, 57–97).

that are initially assigned either to the stars and seen to be the starting points for individual human souls (and those of animals and plants eventually) or to the nine planets as "guardians of time."

Plotinus' understanding of Plato was that the intelligible world is comprised of three "Hypostases" (this was made a technical term by Porphyry[3]), the One, Intellect and Soul.[4] Soul, the third Hypostasis, stands as genus (as a Form to particulars) to the two species of individual soul, the soul of the cosmos and human individual souls, which are given equal status as "sisters," but with the soul of the cosmos enjoying senior status, as Plotinus tells us at IV.3.6.13. Soul the Hypostasis does not descend, and is not therefore the primary concern of this treatise. Nor is it easy to find Soul the Hypostasis in Plato's writings.

First, then, there is the soul of the cosmos, which he refers to variously as the soul of the whole, the soul of the all, all soul etc. He also on occasion refers to "universal soul" *(hê pasa psukhê)*, where he seems to blur the distinction between Soul the Hypostasis and the soul of the cosmos in its higher levels.[5] Secondly there are souls of individuals. Plato tells us in *Timaeus*

[3] See Atkinson (1985, 55).

[4] For a succinct account see O'Meara (1993).

[5] For a fuller discussion of this point see Blumenthal: Soul, World-Soul and Individual Soul in Plotinus (1971).

that the divine craftsman went on to create, from the same materials as the soul of the cosmos (being, sameness and difference), individual souls, although he himself created only the immortal rational part which has the same cognitive powers as the soul of the cosmos—understanding, knowledge, belief and judgement—although less pure (41d–42e), leaving the lesser gods to create the lower irrational parts (69c3).[6] This passage in *Timaeus* may well lie behind Plotinus' claim in chapter 8 of this treatise, that some part of the rational part of the soul remains permanently in the intelligible world. *Timaeus* 90b1 and 90c4 tells us that the highest part of the human soul is divine; but whether this higher part was divided in the way that Plotinus suggests, with part inside and part outside us during our lifetime, seems not to have been a question that Plato himself contemplated, but was left to later Platonists to tussle with.[7] The doctrine of the tripartite soul is familiar from elsewhere in Plato, especially *Republic* (434dff.), where the three elements in the state—guardians, auxiliaries, workers—are likened to the three parts of the human soul—rational, spirited, appetitive. In this treatise Plotinus is particularly concerned with the highest part of the human soul, the

[6] Alcinous *Didaskalikos* 178,24 questions whether Plato believed that the irrational parts of the soul are immortal; see Dillon (1993, 154–155).

[7] See further Archer-Hind (1888, 339, note on line 8).

rational, and it is its cross-over from the intelligible to the sensible world that prompts Plotinus to ask the questions posed at the outset of the treatise. When Plotinus is initially talking about his own experience, this cross-over, or "descent" occurs during the lifetime of the individual human, but the discussion broadens to include the rebirth into a human body of the soul after death.

In what follows I have adopted the position that there are three levels of soul—the Hypostasis and its two species, the soul of the cosmos and individual human (and animal) souls.

Plato—despite the misgivings sounded by Socrates at *Apology* 40c4—firmly believed in the immortality and reincarnation of the human soul, a belief that he is commonly supposed to have derived largely from the Pythagoreans. He states his ideas most clearly in the Myth of Er in *Republic* 10, developing the "Recollection" arguments in *Meno* (81a10ff.) and *Phaedo* (70c5ff and 72e1ff).[8] Plotinus follows Plato in firmly believing in reincarnation, although here too he sees problems, for example whether the individual retains his or her identity between lives.[9] That is not an issue that he raises in this treatise, and it is left undetermined just who is descending as the discussion broadens out. But,

8 At *Phaedrus* 245c–246a and 248d–249d respectively Plato states his belief in the immortality of the soul and its reincarnation.

9 See further Gerson (1994, 76).

as we have seen, in chapter 8 he adds a conviction of his own, that some part of our soul remains always in the Intelligible World, so by the end of the treatise we are back to where we were at the outset, the ascent and descent of the individual soul during the course of a single lifetime. It should be noted that Plato himself does not always give the same account of the soul; for example in the *Phaedo* the soul is envisaged as unitary rather than tripartite, while in *Phaedrus* and *Timaeus* the tripartition of the soul is subordinated to a bipartition between the rational and irrational parts.

In sum, then, Plotinus is in full agreement with Plato that the human soul has three parts, the highest of which is the rational part, which can commune with the divine; that this part of the soul is immortal; and that at times it descends into the body.

The Ascent of the Soul

There are several passages where Plato talks of the ascent of the soul, and these are clearly much in Plotinus' mind as he addresses the issues he has raised. In each case the goal is assimilation *(homoiôsis)* to the highest good in the intelligible world.

Republic

The central books of *Republic* are concerned with the nature and the education of the would-be rulers of the just state, the philosopher kings. A small number of candidates, both male and female, are chosen by aptitude from the whole population. They must first and foremost have a real yearning for philosophical truth, and then a range of characteristics such as bravery, high-mindedness, an aptitude to learn and a good memory. After an initial period of mental and physical education, which they share with other children, they proceed to a lengthy and rigorous form of higher education, through mathematics (which includes arithmetic, plane and solid geometry, astronomy and harmonics) and dialectic. Plotinus discusses the nature of dialectic in I.3.4–5; Thomas Taylor gives a succinct summary: "The dialectic of Plato, which is here discussed, is not the same with that dialectic which is the subject of opinion, and is accurately investigated in the *Topics* of Aristotle. For the former is irreprehensible and most expeditious; since it is connate with things themselves, and employs a multitude of powers in order to the attainment of truth. It likewise imitates intellect, from which it receives its principles, and ascends through well-ordered gradations to real being itself. It also terminates the wanderings of the soul about the sensible; and explores every thing by methods which cannot be confuted, till it arrives at the ineffable principle of things. The business, likewise, of this first of sciences is to employ definitions, divisions, analyzations, and demonstrations, as primary sciences in the investigation of causes; imitating the progression of beings from the first principle of things, and their continual conversion to it as the ultimate object of desire."[10]

There follows a period of fifteen years devoted to gaining practical experience in the lower levels of government, by which time he (or she) has reached the age of fifty. Then, "when they have reached the age of fifty those who have survived safely and have proved themselves superior in every respect and in every point, in both practical and intellectual tasks, must be brought to completion and forced to raise the radiant light of the soul to gaze at that which sheds light on all things. When they have seen the Good itself, they must use it as a standard, and organise the city—both the individuals in it and themselves." (*Republic* 450a2ff). Thereafter they spend their time alternating between further philosophical study and periods of government—in the ascent to and the descent from the intelligible region—before departing to the Isles of the Blest.

The progress of the philosopher is graphically illustrated by the simile of the cave in *Republic* 7.514aff. We are asked to imagine an underground cave that has a long passage leading up to the outside world. Prisoners

---

[10] *The Select Works of Plotinus* (1895, 14n1). Thomas Taylor (1758–1835) was the first to translate the works of Plato and Aristotle, along with those of many Neoplatonists, into English. He was an important influence on thinkers such as Mary Wallstonecraft and the poets Blake, Shelley and Wordsworth. *The Select Works of Plotinus* was published posthumously.

are seated in the cave, shackled in such a way as to be able to see only the wall of the cave furthest from the entrance. Behind and above them, out of their sight, is a low wall, and behind that a fire is burning. Between the wall and the fire men are carrying statues and other images, whose shadows are projected onto the back wall of the cave. The prisoners, who have never seen anything else, assume that these shadows constitute reality; so too with any sounds made by those carrying the images. One of the prisoners is released and forced to turn round and walk towards the entrance. He is dazzled by the firelight and is reluctant to believe that the statues are the source of the unreal shadows, and wants to return to his former state of ignorance. He is then led out of the cave into the outside sunlight, where his eyes become gradually accustomed to the sunlight, so that at first he can bear to look only at shadows and reflections, then at the objects of which these are shadows and reflections, then at the stars in the night sky, and finally at the sun itself. He is then compelled to re-enter the cave, where not only are his eyes filled with darkness but he is also ridiculed by his former fellow-prisoners when he tries to explain to them the true nature of things.

Plato then offers an explanation of the allegory (517a8ff). The released prisoner is the philosopher-king; the cave is the sensible world; the upward journey is the education of the philosopher-king; the outside world is the intelligible world; the shadows, reflections and stars are the Forms; and the sun is the Form of the Good. (How exact the parallel is, is a matter of some dispute; but the broad outlines are undisputed.) At 613a7, just before recounting the Myth of Er, Socrates says "Anyone who is ready and willing to become just, and in the practice of virtue to become like god, as far as is possible for a human, will never be neglected by the gods." The phrase "to become like god as far as is possible for a human" echoes the language of *Theaetetus* 176b (see below) and *Timaeus* 90c2.

Important for Plotinus here are: the *upward* ascent of the philosopher; the toilsome nature of his progress; his ultimate achievement of the vision of the Good; his becoming like God; the need for him to return periodically to the world of his fellow men; and the darkness and the prison-like qualities of the cave. According to the scheme Socrates outlines in *Republic* 7, the philosopher returns to take a minor role in the state after his years of higher education at the age of thirty-five; after fifteen years, at the age of fifty, he is allowed to return to a life of pure philosophy with periodic returns to the society of men as a fully-fledged philosopher-king. So there are two stages in the descent. One takes place when the philosopher has completed his training, and initially ascending by means of hypotheses has, at the age of fifty, comprehended the non-hypothetical first principle of all things. This is described at 532a5 "When a person attempts, by means of dialectic divorced entirely from the senses, using reason to arrive at what each thing is in itself, and not to cease until he has grasped in pure thought just what the Good is." From here he descends back into the realm of dialectic, where he reaches a conclusion (551b6ff). Socrates is at pains to point out that this all takes place entirely in the intelligible world (511c1–2). The second stage of the descent takes place when the philosopher re-enters the sensible world, and it is this stage that Plotinus is concerned with in this treatise.

However, one aspect of Plato's account has caused general concern, and this might well be among the features that Plotinus finds problematic and which at least in part lies behind this treatise. The philosopher is compelled to leave the cave, and when he has achieved his vision of the Good he is forced to return to the cave to live a life that is inferior to the life of pure philosophy that he might otherwise enjoy. Plato's explanation is that the philosopher must pay back to society the debt he owes for his education; the good of the state must supersede the good of the individual. That is part and parcel of justice. But the note of compulsion is a strong one, and the compulsion is applied through the laws by the founders of the state (519c8). This compulsion certainly applies to the first tour of duty between the ages of thirty five and fifty; however at 520eff. he suggests that there will be a greater degree of willingness on the part of the philosopher-kings to undertake subsequent returns. In Plotinus' own case there was clearly little possibility for him or any other philosopher to take part in the government of the Roman world, and we would have to say that the compulsion for him to "descend into bodies" would be a personal rather than a civic moral compunction.[11] Porphyry tells us that Plotinus was involved in public life in that several senators attached themselves to him (*VP* 7), and in private life in that he took into his house the children of bereaved women (*VP* 9). At *Republic* 520b1ff. Plato allows for the fact that in other states there will be no active role in government available to philosophers.

Phaedrus

At *Phaedrus* 246a3ff. Socrates compares the soul to a chariot team consisting of a charioteer and two horses, clearly mirroring the tripartite soul of *Republic* 434d2ff.; the charioteer is the rational part, the two horses are the appetitive and the spirited parts. The horses and the charioteer of the gods are noble and of noble breed, while there is conflict between the two horses of the human

[11] Socrates, at *Theaetetus* 173e1ff., depicts the true philosopher as ranging the places "below the earth and above the heavens" with his mind while keeping his body in the city. This seems to be a reference to *Apology* 18b5–8 where Socrates talks of his critics reviling him for just this sort of enquiry; Sedley (2004, 71ff.) gives references to other works of Plato. This may be the basis of Plotinus' claim in chapter 8 of this treatise that some part of us remains forever in the Intelligible World.

soul, resulting in a difficult and tiresome ride. The soul is winged, but only the souls of the gods are immortal and climb upwards to govern the cosmos, while the souls of humans lose their wings (or feathers) and sink downwards until they seize on something solid, the body, and as a conjoint with the body become mortal, although the soul as a tripartite whole is immortal, as is the case with the gods.[12] The souls of the gods, in a formation led by Zeus, range the heavens, each attending to his or her concerns, attended by those other souls who will or can accompany them—presumably those of lesser gods and some humans. On some occasions the gods soar even higher to the outer rim of the heavens and are carried round with its revolutions, viewing with their mind's eye, "the soul's pilot," the Forms such as justice, moderation, beauty and (non-discursive) knowledge. They are followed by those human souls that are "best able to follow and are most godlike." These souls are enabled to escape the cycle of rebirth *either* permanently, as at 248c3; "This is the ordinance of Fate, that any soul that keeps company with God and sees something of the truth remains beyond harm until the next cycle, and if it can always do this it always remains beyond harm," and at 249a1 where we are told that the true philosopher can eventually escape the cycle of rebirth altogether, *or* at least for a lengthy period, as at *Republic*

[12] For a full discussion of this point see Ferrari (1987, 130–132).

614d7 and 619d5. Others, because of the unruly nature of the team of horses, are able to glimpse the Forms only sporadically and imperfectly before shedding their wings and plunging back downwards again to join the cycle of rebirth. Other souls never even make it that far, but remain below "feeding on opinion." Throughout the myth there is interplay between the timeless character of the life of the gods and the temporality of the course of the human souls; the souls of "those best able to follow . . . and the most godlike," i.e., philosophers, move from one realm to the other. So in this myth Plato is emphasizing that human intellectual activity is, at its best, on a level with that of the gods, and that being godlike (human souls are made of the same stuff as that of the soul of the cosmos, as we are told at *Timaeus* 41d) is a quality achievable by mortals.[13]

There are dissimilarities between this myth and the allegory of the cave in *Republic.* For example the soul of the philosopher has an intense longing to see where the Plain of Truth lies (248b5) and longs to stretch his wings for the upward flight (249d6), and is carried back to earth by the unruly nature of his own soul—there is no external compulsion in either case, as there is in *Republic.* And at 250e1ff. the experience of the philosopher's soul is likened to that of an initiate into a mystery religion, whereas in

[13] See further Ferrari (1987, 131–132), and Hackforth (1952, 69–82) for a commentary on the whole of the myth.

Republic the language is focused on intellectual activity. Nor is it entirely clear whether the *Phaedrus* myth is dealing exclusively with the ascent and descent of the human soul between mortal lives or whether it encompasses also the ascent and descent of the human soul during one mortal lifetime. There is certainly an appeal to the doctrine of Recollection, more familiar from *Phaedo* and *Meno*, at 249c1ff., which is appropriate to rebirth. But both the *Republic* and the *Phaedrus* passages are couched in the form of myth or allegory, and it would be a mistake to seek too close doctrinal similarities or concern ourselves with apparent discrepancies.

For Plotinus the *Phaedrus* myth offers valuable insights into Plato's thought. In particular the distinction between the intelligible world (characterized in *Phaedrus* as colorless, shapeless and intangible, visible only to the intelligence) and the sensible world; the upward journey of the soul; the periodic descent of the human soul to the sensible world; the difficulty of the upward journey; the soul's vision of the Forms; and the escape from the cycle of rebirth for a small number of true philosophers.

Symposium

The myth in *Symposium* offers similar parallels. The dialogue purports to be an account of a symposium held in Athens in 416 BCE at which the guests each offer a speech in praise of Love. The penultimate speech is that of Socrates in which he tells how a woman from

Mantinea called Diotima (the names both suggest divine prophetic revelation) teaches him that "love desires the permanent possession of the good for itself" (206a7), with the ultimate intention of the procreation of true virtue, which is the nearest a man can get to personal immortality. The examples Diotima gives are Lycurgus in Sparta and Solon in Athens, both of whom gave birth to the laws of their country (209d4), wherein lay their immortality. The progress towards this possession is likened to the progress of the initiate into the Eleusinian Mysteries. The initiate will acclimatize himself to all sorts of visible beauty, as it were climbing the rungs of a ladder, then contemplate the invisible beauty of souls, the beauty of the sciences, and the beauty of the single type of knowledge to do with beauty itself, until "in an instant" *(exaiphnês)* he will have a miraculous sight of what is beautiful by its very nature (210e4), a knowledge of the beautiful itself (211c8); the description is clearly that of the Form of the Good. The language throughout is an interweave of the religious and the erotic, as befits the tone of the symposium, and we are left to conclude that the initiated lover will, through intercourse with the Good, beget noble human institutions, as in the case of Lycurgus and Solon. But even though the language is of this character, the progress of the initiate is an intellectual one, and closely mirrors the education of the philosopher in *Republic.* What is perhaps different is that the final revelation is a sudden one, "a moment of truth." The focus here is on the individual in this life—indeed Diotima suggests that there is no immortality other than that of one's legacy—but the implication is that the philosopher will not remain in contemplation, but will "beget" some practical results.[14]

The three passages above are all couched in the form of myth or allegory. Let us now consider four works in which Plato speaks directly.

Letter 7

Plato's seventh letter is addressed to the friends of Dion, the brother-in-law of Dionysius I, ruler of Syracuse, and uncle (and brother-in-law) of his son Dionysius II. Plato had twice visited Sicily as tutor to Dionysius II, and at Dion's instigation these friends wrote to Plato to ask him to make a third visit to Syracuse in 361 BCE. *Letter* 7 is an autobiographical account of this third visit. In it he tells that he was suspicious of Dionysius' motivation and his attitude to philosophy, wondering whether he was truly "fired up by philosophy" (340b2), and that he had advised him of the rigours of the philosophical life. Much of this advice chimes with what is said in *Republic*, *Phaedrus* and *Symposium*. "If a pupil is truly philosophical, in tune with and worthy of the subject, being divine, he considers that he has been told about a miraculous road" (340c1). Philosophy requires

14 See further Rowe (1998, 192–202).

a lifetime's devotion; "it is not something that can be communicated in words like other fields of knowledge, but results from association and cohabitation with the subject itself, and just like a light that is kindled when a spark jumps, it comes to birth in the soul in an instant, and then provides its own nourishment" (341c5). Two points of particular note are (i) that the philosopher is "divine" (*theios* 340c3), an echo of *Phaedrus* 248a1, and (ii) that the final vision of the Good comes "in an instant" (*exaiphnês* 341c7), an echo of *Symposium* 210e4.[15]

Phaedo

Phaedo is named after the narrator of the dialogue, Phaedo of Elis, an admirer of Socrates, who is in prison in Athens in 399 BCE awaiting his execution the following morning. The topic of the dialogue is the immortality of the human soul, and in two places touches on the importance and effect of philosophy on the soul of the philosopher. First, at 65a9ff. Socrates explains how for a philosopher life on earth is a rehearsal for life after death, when with all bodily distractions gone the soul will be able to contemplate the realities of the intelligible world, which can be approached only by means of pure reason, when "the soul by itself must contemplate realities by

[15] Some doubt has been cast on the authenticity of the *Letters*, but there is general agreement that *Letter* 7 is genuine. If, however, it is spurious, then the author has clearly been drawing on the works cited above. Plotinus appears to consider it a genuine work of Plato.

themselves" (66e1). Only true philosophers are anxious to free the soul from the body. Secondly, at 82b10ff., when Socrates has been talking about the rebirth of the souls of those who have not lived the philosophical life, he says that only philosophers are entirely pure at death and enter into the company of gods, into communion with what is divine, pure and single in form (82e2). Although Socrates has suggested that the philosopher does this only "as best he can," always hindered by the distractions of the body, he also seems to hold out the hope that at least some of us can achieve this goal during our lifetime and so proceed to an untroubled afterlife. And unless we envisage that we automatically die the moment we have achieved this state, we must assume that we can maintain the state at least for a time during our lifetime. So although *Phaedo* is primarily directed towards the transition of the soul from this life to the next, it is also concerned with how we live our lives in this world. This is confirmed at 84b1ff.: "[The soul] thinks it must live in this way as long as it is alive."[16] He reminds us at 114c that "those who have sufficiently purified themselves by philosophy live for the rest of time entirely without bodies, and arrive at a still more beautiful dwelling."

16 See further Fleet (1995, 139): "The *Phaedo* is of course set against the background of the death of Socrates, and the separation of soul from body by death is at the forefront; but that is not to say that some sort of separation, albeit temporary, cannot be achieved in this life."

Timaeus

Towards the end of *Timaeus* the speaker (Timaeus of Locri) talks about the proper care of the soul, a topic that had been at the center of Socrates' thought. In many ways it is a summary of what has been said in *Republic*; here the focus is on the rational part of the soul. "The man who is devoted to the love of learning and true wisdom, and has trained his inner resources most rigorously, must think thoughts that are immortal and divine, if he has grasped the truth. And so far as it is possible for a human nature to share in immortality, he will in no way fail" 90b8 (cf. *Symposium* 212a2–7). "When he has made the part that thinks like the object of its thoughts in accordance with its original nature, and has achieved that likeness, he will gain the fulfilment of that noblest life which is proffered to men by the gods both for the present time and for the future" (90d4). Certainly here the emphasis is on the intellectual progress of the soul, likening it to the divine, and both the restrictions imposed by human nature and the possibility of future bliss are to the fore.

Theaetetus

The subject of the dialogue is ostensibly a definition of knowledge.[17] At 172bff. there is a digression in which Socrates contrasts the absolutism of the true philosopher with the relativism of the man of

[17] For a summary of differing interpretations see Sedley (2004, 4–6).

the world. Since the world must always contain some evil, the philosopher must seek to escape "from Here to There" as quickly as possible; "Escape is becoming as like god as is possible; and to become like god is to become just and holy, along with wisdom" (176b1). his last phrase "along with wisdom" gives a philosophical stiffening, and demonstrates, in Sedley's words (2004, 75), "the convergence of moral understanding and moral improvement" which is "quintessentially Socratic" and (76), "By standing back from it, and eventually acquiring a global god's-eye view of the true nature of justice, one acquires the wisdom that both gives one an understanding of justice as an absolute value, and makes one an authentically just person." Many commentators, including Sedley and Burnyeat, point to this as a seminal passage for later Platonists. It may well be that it was singled out for three reasons. Firstly it is succinct, but allows good scope for a broader consideration of Plato's thought. Secondly it is free of the complications of, and discrepancies within, the mythology of *Phaedrus*, *Symposium* and much of *Republic*. Thirdly it allowed for a more personal approach to philosophy, particularly in contrast to *Republic*.

Aristotle

At *Timaeus* 90aff. Plato, talking about the highest, rational, part of the human soul, says that whoever cherishes that part in the pursuit of learning and true wisdom "will of necessity, if he grasps the truth, have thoughts which are immortal and divine; and as far as it is possible for a human nature to achieve immortality, he will in no way fall short of that . . . and will be happy in the extreme." In his note to 90c1, Archer-Hind (1888) points to Aristotle *Nicomachean Ethics* 1177b30 where he (Aristotle) is extolling the contemplative life as constituting "complete human happiness," provided that the life is not cut short. A man achieves this not *qua* human being, but in virtue of something divine in him; he says (1177b33) "we must, as far as is possible, become immortal." Sedley (1999, 324–328) argues persuasively that Aristotle was profoundly in debt to Plato for this account. In both of these passages the focus is on the contemplative life, with the claim that it is through contemplation that we most nearly achieve immortality—but neither philosopher here makes the stronger claim, that we, or any part of us, *is* immortal.

This coherence between Plato and Aristotle is further underlined by Burnyeat. In *The Aquinas Lecture* 2008, entitled *Aristotle's Divine Intellect*, Burnyeat draws a distinction between the Greek terms *logismos* and *dianoia*, which he translates as "reasoning" and "thought," and *nous* and *noein*, which he renders as "intellect" and "understand," particularly *theorêtikos nous*, all of which get their fullest discussion from Aristotle in *De Anima* III 4–8. Reasoning and thought (in the sense of discursive thinking) belong properly to the human soul, while intellect and understanding belong to God. Understanding consists in grasping the intelligible form, the essence which explains the kind and is the starting point of explanatory deductions. They are "part and pinnacle of a whole explanatory system." Divine *nous* alone can function without body, but it can come to reside in a human body; Burnyeat, drawing on *De Anima* 1.4 408b11–29, says "*nous* unlike ordinary thought, is divine and immortal; it can come to reside *in* a human being as itself an extra kind of substance, and it remains completely unaffected by the death of its temporary human vehicle"; and in note 33 "*to theôrein* (contemplation) in mortal humans is the intermittent exercise of the dispositional understanding called *to noein*; they are one and the same state at two levels of actuality." After a lengthy discussion of the way that Aristotle employs his distinctions between first and second potentiality, and first and second actuality, and their application to human and divine intellect, in *De Anima*, he concludes by discussing the passage noted above from *Nicomachean Ethics*; "Finally, it is because God's life in contemplation is the best mode of existence in the universe, and the most pleasant, that for us humans too cognitive activity is the most pleasant: not just noetic contemplation, but also states that God does not share such as waking and perceiving, hopes and memories. What is special about the exercise of *nous*, the highest form of cognition that humans can obtain, is that it is no longer more or less a distant imitation of the divine life. It is a limited span of the very same activity as God enjoys for all time."

So although Plotinus does not appear to have the works of Aristotle to the fore in this treatise, there is a remarkable convergence on this particular issue between Plato, Aristotle and himself.

The Middle Platonists

Platonism after Plato had a complex history with many and varied deviations from the Platonism that Plotinus was seeking to re-establish. This is not the place to trace its development—this has been admirably done by Dillon in *The Middle Platonists* (Duckworth, 1977). It seems that it was Eudorus of Alexandria (fl. c. 25 BCE) who moved Platonism away from the Stoicizing influence of Antiochus of Ascalon (fl. c. 90 BCE) towards a more Pythagorean metaphysic. Eudorus established "assimilation to the divine" as the goal (*telos*) of human life. Dillon (1977, 44), talking of Eudorus, says "this formula remained the distinctive Platonic definition of the *telos* ever afterwards." Other Middle Platonists following in this vein were Plutarch (c. 50–120 CE) and Apuleius of Madaurus (b. c. 125 CE), but the most significant for our purposes was Alcinous (? 2nd century CE). Alcinous is the author of the *Didaskalikos*, an instructional handbook of the doctrines of Plato. Porphyry (*VP* 14) says of Plotinus that "in his works both Stoic and Peripatetic doctrines are interwoven, although they lie under the surface," and this is true also of the *Didaskalikos*, which thereby offers an interesting insight into the practices of the philosophical schools of the period. In chapter 28, Alcinous addresses directly the issue of "assimilation to god as far as is possible," quoting and discussing a range of Platonist authors. At 181,43 H he says "the goal would be assimilation to god—obviously the god in the heavens and not, of course, the god above the heavens." Alcinous has in chapter 10 (164,18 ff. H) already drawn this distinction. Dillon (1993, 103), commenting on this passage, sees Alcinous as positing a cosmic triad of a world soul, an intellect of this world soul (otherwise described as "intellect of the whole heaven")—which is to be reckoned as a distinct entity—and a First Cause, which is also still an intellect (modelled on Aristotle's Unmoved Mover of *Metaphysics* 12). It is the second of these that Alcinous is pointing to in chapter 28. All of this is an interesting foreshadowing of Plotinus. So for Alcinous "assimilation to god" is assimilation to the intellect of the world soul. As Dillon remarks (1993, 300) "To bring the Supreme God into a relationship of likeness with man would be to compromise his transcendence." All this, *mutatis mutandis*, would suggest that in the phrase "at one with the divine" Plotinus is referring not to the first Hypostasis, the One, but to the second Hypostasis, Intellect.

Plotinus

It is now time to turn to Plotinus himself and to outline what "assimilation to the divine" means for him. We should remember that the *Enneads* are Plotinus' written accounts of the seminars that he held after his arrival in Rome in 244 CE. These seminars were based, as his pupil Porphyry tells us (*VP* 3), on his earlier studies of Plato in Alexandria under Ammonius. He started compiling these accounts some ten years later, in 254 CE, when he himself was 50 years old, and they were subsequently edited by Porphyry as the *Enneads*, and it is in this form that they have come down to us. So we can expect not only inconsistencies in Plato to be reflected in the *Enneads*, but also the objections expressed by those attending the seminars. Although Plotinus does not compose formally in Plato's dialogue style, with each speaker identified and the historical setting carefully outlined, the cut and thrust of lively debate is evident, with frequent objections raised and answered. The net result is not so much a "system" as a lively engagement between himself and Plato, which he invites us to join. It is often more rewarding to trace the line of argument vertically back to Plato (often through later writers such as those mentioned by Porphyry at *VP* 14) than laterally to other treatises in the *Enneads*. IV.8 is an exception, however, and is much more a record of Plotinus' private reflections.

One particular feature of Plato's teachings that figures large in Plotinus' writings is the hierarchy within the intelligible world. Plotinus takes further than anyone before him what Plato says at *Republic* 509b7 about the Form of the Good, that "it is not Being, but even beyond Being, surpassing it in majesty and power." He gives it a status transcending the intelligible world—it is named by Porphyry as the First Hypostasis. Furthermore he equates it to the One, reflecting Plato's increasing tendency to mathematize. This move from a moral towards an intellectual concept of deity is reflected in the education of the would-be philosopher-kings in *Republic* 7 which is heavily mathematical in its earlier content (and perhaps too in the later regime of dialectic, whose content Plato says very little about) and is further exemplified in his later works, such as *Philebus* (and perhaps too in the so-called Lecture on the Good), where a moral hierarchy gives way to a mathematical one of increasing pluralization, at the head of which must stand the One.

Given that in all the passages quoted earlier in this *Introduction* Plato makes it clear that the human soul can attain to final knowledge of the highest principles, Plotinus has to be able to accommodate in his writings some more complex understanding of the processes by which that final knowledge, the "assimilation to the divine," is gained.[18]

[18] See further Gerson (1994, ch. 8, sec. 2) for a full discussion of such modes of intellection. See section 4 of Henry's *Introduction: Plotinus' Place in the History of Thought* in MacKenna. xlv–li, and Thesleff (1980) for a discussion of the stages of the ascent.

Since Plotinus characterizes the whole of the Intelligible World as divine there is a wide range of opinion as to (a) what the human soul seeks to become assimilated to—is it the One (the First Hypostasis) or Intellect (the Second Hypostasis)?—and (b) what the nature of the assimilation is—is it unification or identification, with or without loss of individuality, a "mystic union" with the deity, or nothing more than contemplation of the Forms? This is not the place to rehearse the arguments, which have been well dealt with by, among others, Rist (1967, ch. 16), Gerson (1994, ch. 10), Emilsson (2007, 101–103), and O'Meara (1993, ch. 10).

In sum, Plotinus' belief, in my view, is that the human soul in its highest, rational, phase turns back inwards to contemplate its priors—this process is called *epistrophê* by Plotinus, and in the case of the soul can otherwise be termed "ascent." The more centered it becomes (or the higher it ascends) the more it moves from contemplation of plurality to that of unity, and the less discursive its thinking becomes until finally (and "in an instant") its thinking ceases to be discursive and becomes, as it were, a moment of truth outside time. In describing this process Plotinus' vocabulary changes from process words, often with the prefix *dia-*, such as *dianoia* (discursive thinking), to words that denote contact, such as *sunaphê.* This is "assimilation to the divine." At its highest it touches or apprehends the One without itself becoming the One. At VI.9.3.21, Plotinus says: "Hurrying towards the Good, you must ascend to the principle within yourself, become a unity instead of a plurality so as to be a spectator of the Origin and the One. You must become Intellect, entrust and establish your soul under Intellect, so that it may awaken to receive what Intellect sees, and thereby see the One." So I would suggest that the picture presented at the start of IV.8 is of the human soul becoming assimilated to Intellect and engaging with the One by a sort of contact and timeless apprehension. That is the point from which the "descent into bodies" begins.

Note on the Text

LINE NUMBERS IN THE TRANSLATION are approximate and do not always match the original Greek text. Since the commentary follows the sequence of the English translation, there may sometimes be a slight discrepancy in the ordering.

The Greek text adopted is that of the Oxford edition. Deviations from the text are noted in the commentary. Each *Ennead* is referred to by Roman numerals, followed by the number of the treatise, the chapter of the treatise, and, finally, separated by a comma, the line number or numbers, e.g, V.1.3, 24–27.

It is customary to add the chronological number given by Porphyry in his *Life of Plotinus (Vita Plotini)*, so that, for example, V.1. is designated V.1 [10]. In this series the chronological number is given only where it is of significance for Plotinus' philosophical stance. The following charts indicate the chronological order.

It should be noted that Plotinus did not provide titles to the treatises and that these were later added by Porphyry when preparing his edition from those that had become traditional amongst the readers of Plotinus' manuscripts (see Porph *VP* 4), although Porphyry himself sometimes gives different titles to the same treatise in his chronological *VP* 4–6) and thematic (*VP* 24–25) lists, and variant titles are also found in Simplicius and Philoponus in the 6th century.

Chronological Order of the *Enneads*

Enn.		*Enn.*		*Enn.*		*Enn.*		*Enn.*		*Enn.*	
I.1	**53**	II.1	**40**	III.1	**3**	IV.1	**21**	V.1	**10**	VI.1	**42**
I.2	**19**	II.2	**14**	III.2	**47**	IV.2	**4**	V.2	**11**	VI.2	**43**
I.3	**20**	II.3	**52**	III.3	**48**	IV.3	**27**	V.3	**49**	VI.3	**44**
I.4	**46**	II.4	**12**	III.4	**15**	IV.4	**28**	V.4	**7**	VI.4	**22**
I.5	**36**	II.5	**25**	III.5	**50**	IV.5	**29**	V.5	**32**	VI.5	**23**
I.6	**1**	II.6	**17**	III.6	**26**	IV.6	**41**	V.6	**24**	VI.6	**34**
I.7	**54**	II.7	**37**	III.7	**45**	IV.7	**2**	V.7	**18**	VI.7	**38**
I.8	**51**	II.8	**35**	III.8	**30**	IV.8	**6**	V.8	**31**	VI.8	**39**
I.9	**16**	II.9	**33**	III.9	**13**	IV.9	**8**	V.9	**5**	VI.9	**9**

	Enn.		*Enn.*		*Enn.*		*Enn.*		*Enn.*		*Enn.*
1	I.6	**10**	V.1	**19**	I.2	**28**	IV.4	**37**	II.7	**46**	I.4
2	IV.7	**11**	V.2	**20**	I.3	**29**	IV.5	**38**	VI.7	**47**	III.2
3	III.1	**12**	II.4	**21**	IV.1	**30**	III.8	**39**	VI.8	**48**	III.3
4	IV.2	**13**	III.9	**22**	VI.4	**31**	V.8	**40**	II.1	**49**	V.3
5	V.9	**14**	II.2	**23**	VI.5	**32**	V.5	**41**	IV.6	**50**	III.5
6	IV.8	**15**	III.4	**24**	V.6	**33**	II.9	**42**	VI.1	**51**	I.8
7	V.4	**16**	I.9	**25**	II.5	**34**	VI.6	**43**	VI.2	**52**	II.3
8	IV.9	**17**	II.6	**26**	III.6	**35**	II.8	**44**	VI.3	**53**	I.1
9	VI.9	**18**	V.7	**27**	IV.3	**36**	I.5	**45**	III.7	**54**	I.7

Synopsis

Chapter 1

1–10 Question: I often wake up to my true self and become at one with the divine. So why do I ever descend back to my body?

10–22 Heraclitus, Empedocles and the Pythagoreans offered little clarity on this question.

22–25 Perhaps Plato can enlighten us, although even he is not entirely consistent.

26–41 In some works he disparages the sensible world and the association of soul with body.

41–50 But in *Timaeus* he calls the material cosmos an intelligent god, endowed with soul by a benign demiurge, along with all living creatures.

Chapter 2

1–14 Questions:

- (i) Why in general does soul associate with body?
- (ii) What is the nature of the material cosmos?
- (iii) Is the soul in the cosmos willingly or by necessity?
- (iv) Has its maker acted correctly, or like individual souls that sink deep into bodies in order to prevent the dissipation of their constituent parts?

14–19 Answer: The cosmos is perfect and needs only the lightest touch on the helm.

19–26 Individual souls can withdraw from the body and share in the perfection of the world soul, but still show providential care for the body.

26–38 There are two sorts of caring:

- (i) disengaged, as the care of the divine soul for the whole cosmos, which leaves the carer uncontaminated, and
- (ii) engaged care, where the carer is infected by the act of caring.

38–53 Question: What about the souls of the stars?

Answer: They operate like the world soul, free of the faults of individual souls such as lack of intellection, appetites, fears and desires; they are not drawn earthwards, but are turned towards the higher realm.

Chapter 3

1–6 The human soul suffers all kinds of affections in the body. But Plato's views on the descent of the soul are not inconsistent with his views on universal soul.

6–16 Universal Intellect contains individual powers and intellects just as a genus includes species and universal Soul includes individual souls. Universal Intellect exists in the intelligible world whole and entire, but includes actualized individual intellects.

16–21 In just the same way the lives of individual citizens perfect the life of the city, and individual fires perfect universal fire.

21–30 The function of rational soul is more than intellection; it organizes and directs the sensible world, which is the necessary outcome of the intelligible world.

Chapter 4

1–5 The individual soul turns back to its intelligible source but also directs its powers downwards.

5–10 But as long as it remains with universal Soul, directing the intelligible world or the heavens, it is untroubled.

10–24 When it no longer looks to the intelligible world but to the partial material world, it sets itself apart and is weakened; it deserts the universal and cares only for the particular outside itself, sinking deep into the body. It loses its wings and no longer shares in directing the cosmos.

24–28 It is ensnared, entombed in the body, acting not through intellect but through the senses.

28–31 But it can turn back to intellection, freeing itself from its chains, and ascend to the contemplation of real beings through recollection. It always retains something of the transcendent.

31–42 So an individual soul has a double life, partly in the intelligible world, partly in the sensible world, as Plato implies in *Timaeus*.

Chapter 5

1–8 There is no inconsistency in the various words and phrases used by Plato, Empedocles and Heraclitus, although some stress the voluntary, others the involuntary nature of the soul's descent.

8–16 Nothing goes to a worse situation voluntarily, but as a necessary punishment for voluntary wrongdoing. But when it brings benefit to the lower order it can be said that the god, as the primary cause of all things, sent it down.

16–24 The soul's error is twofold:

(i) in initiating its descent; the punishment lies in the pain of the descent

(ii) in acting wrongly in the sensible world; the punishment for lesser wrongdoing is successive rebirth, while greater wrongdoing earns severer retribution.

24–27 So although the soul is divine, it descends into bodies—

(i) through its own wilfulness

(ii) through its power to organise the sensible world.

27–35 If it returns quickly, no harm is done to it by its engagement with the sensible world. Its deeds and powers would have remained latent in the intelligible world. Actuality brings to light what would otherwise remain hidden.

35–37 We marvel at the inner reality when we see the outer richness of the cosmos.

Chapter 6

1–6 Souls and the contents of the intelligible world are the necessary product of the One.

6–10 Similarly souls of necessity produce the contents of the sensible world, since it is the nature of all things to generate their posteriors.

10–18 Soul remains itself and produces its posteriors by some ineffable power that cannot remain circumscribed but of necessity continues to produce until all things are fully actualized, sharing in the nature of the good to the limits of their ability.

18–23 Matter has either always existed or is a necessary outcome of prior causes. In either case it is not isolated, but participates in the good.

23–28 The relationship between the intelligible and the sensible worlds is not reciprocal, though they are eternally bound together. The sensible world is a manifestation of the intelligible, and derives its being by imitating the intelligible, which exists by its own nature.

Chapter 7

1–6 The soul has a twofold nature; it has its being on the fringe of the intelligible world, but borders on and of necessity partakes in the sensible world. It should be satisfied with this intermediate rank.

6–17 It both gives to the sensible world, and takes from it if it becomes embroiled in it. But it can reemerge and use its experience of the sensible world to gain a clearer knowledge of the good by comparison with its opposite. Some souls, being weaker, need to actually experience evil in order to understand the good more clearly.

17–22 Intellect, in its outgoing phase, cannot move upwards but only downwards to what is immediately below it, soul, to which it hands on the baton before returning upwards.

23–32 Similarly individual souls direct their activity downwards to the sensible world, but can then return upwards to a vision of the intelligible. The soul of the cosmos by contrast does not become embroiled in the sensible world, and has no direct experience of evil; it remains in eternal contemplation of its priors. But it cannot, in that it is soul, escape bestowing benefits on the sensible world.

Chapter 8

1–6 A part of the individual soul always remains in the intelligible world. The embroilment of the individual soul in the sensible world makes us unaware of the contemplation of this part.

6–13 For we know what is occurring in any one part of the soul only when it is perceived by the whole soul.

13–17 The world soul acts as a whole on the whole through its lower phase by intellection, and does not become embroiled.

17–22 But individual souls are partial and concerned with the partial, and are thrown into turmoil by alien feelings such as appetites, desires and pleasures.

22–23 But there always remains a part free of such emotions.

Translation of Plotinus Ennead *IV.8 [6]*

1. I often wake up from my body into my true self, so that being within myself and outside all other things I enjoy a vision of wonderful beauty. It is then that I believe most firmly that I am part of the nobler realm, living a life of perfect activity; I have become at one with the divine, | and being securely established in it I have entered into that higher actuality, setting myself above all the rest of the intelligible world. But when, after being at rest in the divine, I have started my descent from intellection to discursive reasoning, I wonder how on earth it is that even now I am descending, and how on earth it is that my soul has come to be in my body, since it has been revealed | to be what it is in itself, despite being in the body.

Heraclitus,[19] who urged us to enquire into this question, offered such phrases as "necessary changes between

[19] DK 60, 84a, 84b, 101.

opposites" and "the way up is the way down" and "what changes is at repose" and "weariness is to toil and to be making a start at the same things." He left us to make our own conjectures, | since he chose not to make his argument clear to us—perhaps because a person must search within himself, just as he found the answer by searching it out by himself.

Empedocles[20] too, who said that it is a law that souls who have sinned must fall into this world, and that he himself came here "as an exile from the divine, obedient to maddened strife," disclosed just as little, in my opinion, | as Pythagoras and his followers who spoke in riddles about this and many other questions; but Empedocles' lack of clarity is also due to the fact that he writes in verse.

We are left with the divine Plato,[21] who has said in many places in his works many noble things about the soul and its arrival here, | so that we can hope for some clarity from him.

So what does this philosopher say?

It is clear that he does not always speak with sufficient consistency for us to make out his intentions with any

20 DK 115, lines 13–14.

21 *Phaedo* 67d; *Cratylus* 400c; *Phaedo* 62b; *Republic* 514a, 515c, 517b; *Phaedrus* 246c, 247d, 249a; *Republic* 619d; *Timaeus* 34b.

ease. But he always holds the whole of the sensible world in low esteem, and censures the association of the soul with the body, saying that the soul "is in fetters" and "is entombed in the body" | and that "the secret saying, which claims that the soul is in prison, is a great one." And I think that for him the Cave signifies this world (just as the cavern does for Empedocles[22])—at least when he says that the soul's journey to "the intelligible world" is "a release from its fetters" and "an ascent" out of the Cave. | In *Phaedrus* loss of wings is the cause of the soul's arrival in this world; furthermore he talks of cycles that return the soul, after its ascent, back to this world; and of judgments that despatch other souls down here, and of the casting of lots, and of luck, and of necessity. | In all these cases he is censuring the approach of the soul to body. But in *Timaeus*, when he is speaking of this All, he praises the cosmos and calls it a blessed god; and he says that its soul was bestowed by the demiurge in his goodness so that this All might be intelligent, since it had to be intelligent | and could not be so without soul. So that was the reason why the soul of the All was sent by the god; and the soul of each one of us was sent so that the All might be perfected. For it was necessary that all the same kinds of living creatures should exist in the sensible world as exist in the intelligible. |

[22] DK 120.

2. So that once we have sought to learn about our own soul from Plato, we find we are obliged to grapple with a search about soul in general. How on earth is it in the nature of soul to associate with body? What are we to claim about the nature of a cosmos that soul inhabits, | either willingly or under compulsion or in some other way? As for its maker, has he acted correctly, or has he perhaps acted like our own souls? For since they govern inferior bodies they were bound thereby to sink deep inside them, if they were to control them. For each body would be scattered, swept away to its proper place; | whereas in the All all bodies come by nature to rest in their proper places. Material bodies need much painstaking foresight, since many alien forces attack them and they are always held in the grip of deficiency and need every possible assistance in their great difficulties. But the cosmos is perfect, fully adequate and self-sufficient, | and contains nothing contrary to its nature; so it requires only a brief word of command, as it were; and its soul is always as it wants to be by its nature, free of appetites and affections, "for nothing leaves or is added."

That is why Plato says that our soul, if it is in the company of that perfect soul, | itself reaches perfection, "journeying on high and organizing the whole cosmos"; when it withdraws so as not to be within bodies and not to belong to any one body, then it too, just like the soul of the All, will organize the All with ease. For it is in no way an evil for soul to give body the power of well-being and existence, | because not all providential care taken over an inferior stops the carer from remaining in the best possible state.

For there are two sorts of caring in the totality of things. There is overall caring, on the part of someone organizing by decree with a royal authority that keeps him clear of the action; and there is caring for an individual, where there is already self-actuated engagement and a contact with the operation, which infects the doer | with the nature of the operation. The divine soul is said to control the whole of the heavens in the former way, eternally, remaining aloof in its higher aspect but transmitting its lowest power into the world. But the god could still not be criticized for having produced the soul of the All in something inferior, nor has the soul been deprived of what is in its nature, | since it has this from eternity and will always have it as something that cannot be contrary to its nature, something that belongs to it for ever, without end or beginning.

And when Plato says that the souls of the stars bear the same relation to their bodies as <the soul of the All> does to the All (for he inserts their bodies too "into the circles" of the soul) | he would also be preserving the appropriate well-being of the stars. For there are two reasons why the association of the soul with the body causes it difficulty. First, it inhibits intellection; and secondly, it fills the soul with pleasures, appetites and distress; | in neither case would this happen to a soul that has not sunk inside the body, is not someone's soul, and does not belong to the body (but rather owns the body), and is such as not to need anything nor be defective in anything. Consequently this soul is not filled with appetites or fears, since it will never feel apprehension concerning a body of this kind, | nor does any distraction deflect it downwards and draw it away from the better blessed vision. Rather it is always turned to those higher beings, marshalling the All with a power that remains uninvolved.

3. But the human soul is said to suffer all kinds of distress and harmful affections in the body, where it finds itself beset by follies, desires, fears and the other evils; for the body is its fetter and tomb, and the cosmos its cave and cavern. So let us now state what view Plato has about the soul's descent—a view that does not show any | inconsistency, since the causes are different.

Universal Intellect, then, exists whole and entire in the realm of intellection, which we call the intelligible world. But there also exist the intellective powers included in it, as well as the individual intellects—since Intellect is not just one, but one and many; | and there had to be many souls as well as one soul, and these many souls had to be distinct, stemming from the one soul, just as species stem from a single genus, some better, others worse, some more intellective, others less intellective in actuality. For there, in Intellect, there is one thing—Intellect including everything else by its power like a great living creature; | and there are too the beings that Intellect included by its power, each one existing in actuality. It is just as if a living city included other living beings; the life of the city would be more complete and powerful, but nothing would stop the other lives from sharing the same nature. Or it is as if both a great fire and small fires stemmed from a universal fire; universal | being is the being of universal fire, or rather the being from which the being of universal fire stems.

The function of the more rational soul is intellection, but not only intellection. For otherwise in what way would it differ from intellect? For it took on something extra, in addition to being intellective, so that it did not remain just intellect. And it too | has a function, as does everything that exists in the intelligible world. It looks to what is prior to it and has intellection of it; but when it looks into itself it has intellection of what is posterior to it, which it organizes and directs, and controls it. For it was impossible for the totality of beings in the intelligible world to remain static when it was possible for something else to come into being in succession to it—something that is inferior but which has to exist if what is prior to it exists. |

4. In turning back to their source, individual souls experience a yearning that is intellective, but they also have a power directed to the world below—just like light, which depends on the sun above but is unstinting in its generosity to what comes after it. As long as | these souls remain in the intelligible world together with universal soul, they are untroubled, and in the heavens they remain together with the universal soul and share with it in directing. They are just like men in the court of an absolute monarch who join with him in directing, without themselves coming down from the palace. For they are then all together in the same place.

But the individual souls | move out of the universal to become partial and to belong to themselves; each of them, as if weary of being with something else, retires into its own place. When it does this over a period of time, fleeing the All and setting itself apart, and does not look at the intelligible—then it becomes a part, is isolated, grows weak, | becomes embroiled and looks to the partial; in its separation from the universal it has mounted a single vehicle and has abandoned everything else; it has come and turned to that one vehicle that is battered by everything on all sides. By now it has deserted the universal, and governs the particular with great difficulty, caring for what is outside itself through contact, | being present in it and sinking deep inside it. This is where it experiences what Plato calls "moulting," and is caught in the fetters of the body, losing the invulnerability of directing the nobler part <of the cosmos> that is enjoyed by the universal soul. It was altogether better for it earlier on when it had soared back upwards. | So it has been ensnared, having fallen and become entangled in chains; it acts by sense since it is prevented from acting by intellect as it originally did; it is said to have become entombed, to be in a cave—but when it turns to intellection it is said to be freed from its chains and to ascend, when it starts "to contemplate real beings" by recollection. | For in spite of everything it always keeps something in some way transcendent. So souls come to have two lives, so to speak, forced to live one life "there" and one "here," turn and turn about. Those more able to consort with Intellect live more of their life "there," while those in the opposite state, either by nature or chance, live more of their life "here." | Plato tacitly implies this when he makes a division in the contents of the second mixing bowl and distinguishes them as parts, saying that at this point they had to enter into becoming, since they had become parts of a particular kind. And if he says that god "sowed" them he must be understood to be speaking in the same way as when he has him talk and make declarations. | For his explanation generates and creates things that exist in the nature of universals, bringing forward one after another things that are everlastingly coming into being in this way and that are everlastingly existing, to make his exposition clear.

5. There is no inconsistency in Plato's "sowing seed for birth," "the descent for the perfection of the world," "judgment," "the cave," "necessity," "volition" (for necessity includes volition), and "being in the body which is something evil"; or in Empedocles' "flight | from god," "the wandering" and "the sin which brings judgment"; or in Heraclitus' "repose consisting in flight"; nor, generally speaking, is there a discrepancy between the voluntary and the involuntary nature of the descent. For everything that goes to the worse does so unwillingly; but even so, when it goes by its innate momentum, in suffering what is worse it is said to be experiencing justice for what it has done. But | whenever it becomes necessary to act and be acted upon eternally in this way by the law of nature, and when, descending from what is above it, it encounters and serves the need of another in its progress, then one would not be speaking inconsistently with the truth or with oneself in saying that a god had sent it down. For even if there are many | intervening stages, the final outcome of each chain of events is referred to the starting point.

The error of the soul is twofold. On the one hand it lies in the cause of its descent, on the other in acting wrongly when it has arrived down here. The penalty in the former case is just this—what it has suffered after descending. In the latter the lesser punishment consists of sinking into further bodies in quick succession, depending on the judgement of what it deserves, | (that this happens by divine decree is made clear by the word "judgment") while excessive degrees of vice are considered to deserve severer punishment under the direction of avenging deities.

So although the soul is something divine and comes from the higher realm, | it comes to reside in the body; although it is a god, albeit of lower status, it comes down here in this way through self-willed inclination, because of its power and its intention to organize its posteriors. If it escapes quickly, it will have suffered no damage by acquiring a knowledge of evil, by having learnt about the nature of vice, by bringing its powers into the open and by displaying its functions and actions, | which would have remained latent in the immaterial world and would have been meaningless, forever failing to come to actuality. The soul itself would never have known the powers that it possessed, since they would not have been brought to light or issued forth. For actuality revealed everywhere the power that would have remained utterly hidden, blotted out, so to speak, and not existing since it never truly existed. | For now each one of us, seeing the outer richness, marvels at the inner reality and the creation of such subtleties.

6. So there must be not only a unity, because otherwise all things would have been hidden within it, lacking shape; and not even one of the real beings would exist if it remained within itself, static. Nor would there be the plurality of those beings generated from the One if the beings that came after them had not issued from them | to take the rank of souls.

In just the same way there could not, of necessity, be just souls without their products coming to light, since it belongs to every nature to produce its posteriors and to unfold itself, as from a seed, from some undivided starting point that proceeds to an outcome in the sensible world. | What is prior remains for ever in its proper abode, while what is posterior is engendered, so to speak, by some ineffable power, as great as the power that resides in the beings "up there," a power that could not remain static like someone who has jealously drawn a circle round himself. Rather it had to move forward ceaselessly until all things reached the ultimate limits of their potential, driven by a power, limitless in every direction, that sends them out from within itself | and cannot leave anything without a share in itself. For there was nothing to prevent anything, whatever it was, from having a share in the nature of good to the extent that each thing had the ability to participate.

If, then, the nature of matter always existed, it was impossible for it not to participate, because of its very existence, in that which bestows | the good on everything to the extent that each thing can receive it. Or else, if the coming to be of matter was a necessary consequence of prior causes, not even in this case did it need to exist in isolation as if that which grants being like some favor had come to a halt before reaching it because of some inability. So the very great beauty of the sensible world is a manifestation | of all that is most noble in the intelligible, of its power and goodness. All things that exist, both in the intelligible world and the sensible world, are for ever bound together—the intelligibles by their own nature, the sensibles receiving their being eternally by participation in them, imitating the intelligible nature to the best of their ability.

7. Because this nature is twofold, both intelligible and sensible, it is better for the soul to have its being in the intelligible world; but even so, since it has the sort of nature that it has, it must of necessity have the ability to participate in the sensible world as well, and it should not feel aggrieved with itself, in that it is not

superior in all respects, | for holding a middle rank among real beings.

It belongs to the divine realm. But since it is on the fringe of the intelligible world and borders on the sensible nature, it must give something of itself to this world, but is also bound to receive something back from it, if ever it should not organize with the secure part of itself but sink into the interior with excessive eagerness, | not remaining whole along with the whole. Most particularly, it is possible for it to emerge again having gained some record of what it saw and experienced "here," and having understood what existence "there" is like. By comparing what are in a way opposites it in a way understands more clearly the nobler things. For experience of evil amounts to a clearer understanding of good | for those whose powers are too weak for them to know with real understanding what evil is before experiencing it.

Just as the outward progress of Intellect is a descent to the limit of what is inferior—for it cannot ascend to the transcendent, but must act outwards from itself, and since it cannot remain | within itself, it must by the law of nature come to be soul; this is its end, and it must hand over to soul what comes next in order while it itself rises swiftly back upwards. Of just the same nature is the activity of soul; what is posterior to it is this world, and what is prior to it is its vision of real beings. This sort of experience happens in time | to souls that are in division and in an inferior situation, when a reversion towards the superior occurs. By contrast, what is called the soul of the cosmos has not even become involved in this inferior activity, but has no experience of evils, but embraces intellectively what is below it in contemplation, although forever depending on its priors. It has both abilities at the same time |—to receive from "there" and to minister to the world "here," since it is inconceivable for it, being soul, not to touch upon this world too.

8. Furthermore—if I may venture to state my convictions more clearly against the opinions of others, as I must—not even our own soul sinks in its entirety, but there is always some part of it in the intelligible world. But if the part in the sensible world wins mastery, or rather is itself mastered and thrown into turmoil, it hinders us from having perception of whatever the higher part of the soul is contemplating. |

For the object of intellection reaches us only when it descends and arrives at the level of perception. For we do not know everything that occurs in any one part of the soul until it reaches the whole soul. For example appetite is not known to us while it remains in the appetitive part of the soul, | but only when we apprehend it with our inner powers of perception or of discursive thought, or both. For every soul has in it something of what is below on the side of the body, and something of what is above on the side of intellect.

The soul that is whole and belongs to the whole brings order to the whole by the part of it that is on the side of the body, transcending it effortlessly, because it acts on what is below it not through calculation, | as we do, but by intellection—for "art does not deliberate"—organizing what is below it, what belongs to the whole. But souls that have become partial and belong to a part, although they too contain the transcendent, are troubled by perception and apprehension when they apprehend many things that are contrary to their nature and that cause them distress and turmoil. For they are concerned with what is partial, | defective, and surrounded by much that is alien and much that arouses desire in them. It has pleasures too, and its pleasure is deceptive. But it has a part that is free of the pleasures of the moment, and this part lives a life of consistency.

Commentary

Chapter 1

IN THIS CHAPTER Plotinus begins by outlining the issue to be discussed in the treatise—how is it that, after having achieved assimilation to the divine, his soul descends back into the body? He then reviews—and rejects—three earlier thinkers, Heraclitus (fl. c. 500 BCE), Empedocles (c. 492–432 BCE) and Pythagoras (fl. c. 500 BCE). He finally, and naturally, turns to Plato and refers to passages in *Phaedo*, *Republic*, *Phaedrus* and *Timaeus*, in which Plato affirms the superiority of the intelligible world over the sensible world, and describes the journeying of the human soul from the one to the other. He then draws a distinction between the arrival of the human soul in the human body and the arrival of the soul of the cosmos in the cosmos. Finally he states that the intention of the god in sending both the soul of the cosmos and the human soul into the sensible world was that it might be perfected.

Lines 1–11

The first sentence of Plotinus' Greek runs right down to line 11 *(. . . despite being in my body)* and is a rare example of Plotinus in an autobiographical mode. He starts by recounting his experiences when he has enjoyed assimilation to the divine (lines 1–7), which implies some degree of memory of the experience. Although Plato expresses some reservations in *Letter* 7 341c and at *Timaeus* 28c about writing down the inner core of his experiences and beliefs since, unlike other branches of knowledge they cannot easily be put into words, he clearly supposes that at least some memory is retained of the consummation of the education of the philosopher-kings in *Republic*, the final revelation given by Diotima in *Symposium* and the vision of the cosmos and its workings attained by the charioteer of the soul in *Phaedrus:* e.g., at *Republic* 534c we are told that the true dialectician "distinguishes in discourse the idea of the Good . . . and knows the Good itself." It is this knowledge of the Good that allows him to revisit the field of dialectic and confirm as truths what had previously been assumptions. But for Plotinus the issue was more complex. With the establishment of the First Hypostasis as something beyond being and beyond intellection ("hyperontic" and "hypernoetic") it was not possible to claim knowledge of the unknowable, and therefore difficult to say in what way it was possible to have memory of an encounter with it. He devotes much space to this topic, notably in *Enneads* IV.3 and IV.4.27–28. Memory is discursive, occurs in time and belongs to the phase of the soul where plurality is involved. That is not to say that we cannot remember that we had the encounter, but we do not remember any content of the encounter. As Gerson (1994, 181) succinctly puts it: "We cannot, as it were, retire momentarily into the chamber of Intellect, snatch a bit of a priori knowledge, and return with it ready to pronounce on some necessity in nature." But that is not to say that an encounter with the inexpressible cannot inform our discursive thinking.

1, 1 *often:* since lines 1–11 comprise a single sentence in Plotinus' Greek, in theory the adverb *often* could qualify *I wonder* (cf. O'Meara 1993, 105), but its position next to the verb *wake up* makes it more natural to assume that the two go together. Porphyry (*VP* 23) says: "His object and aim was to be united and come close to the God who is above all things. During the time that I was with him he achieved this four times in ineffable actuality, not potentiality." Porphyry was with Plotinus for some five years, and this has led some commentators to suspect that *often* is being used loosely by Plotinus. But there is sharper divergence of opinion as to whether Plotinus is describing here union with Intellect or union with the One. Emilsson (2007, 101–103) sides with O'Meara (1993, 104–105) in distinguishing the experience described here in IV.8 (union with Intellect) from that described in VI.9.9–11 (union with the One). To maintain that distinction would preserve the comparative rarity of Plotinus' union with the One and a more frequent union with Intellect. See above Introduction, 39.

1, 1 *I wake up from my body:* Plato himself does not draw on the idea that the embodied soul is asleep, except perhaps at *Republic* 533bc, where he talks about geometry and its allied subjects as part of the curriculum of the philosopher-kings as having some grasp on real being, but only in a dreamlike way as long as the students leave the assumptions they employ undisturbed and without a proper account; and at 534d he talks of the common man as dreaming and sleeping his life away. It is more likely that the idea of the embodied soul asleep came into the Platonic tradition later. Witt (1937, 132) and Dillon (1993, 126) point to Maximus of Tyre's (fl. 152 CE) *Learning and Recollection* 16.1. Plotinus himself uses it on several occasions, e.g., III.6.6, 65 and V.5.11, 19. At *Republic* 476c Plato says that non-philosophers who cannot see Beauty itself are living in a dream.

1, 2 *being within myself:* turning in on oneself was for Plotinus the first step in assimilation to the divine; e.g., at VI.9.7, 17, talking about the approach to the One, he says: "The soul must let go of everything outside itself and turn entirely inwards." The verb *turn (epistrephesthai)* and its cognate noun *epistrophê* are key terms in Plotinus, and are used to refer to the turning inwards of a posterior to its prior (see O'Meara 1993, chs. 6 and 7 for a succinct discussion of the part played by *turning* and its counterpart *emanation* in the derivation of all things). Plotinus uses the verb *epistrephesthai* in just this sense in this treatise at 4.28. The image is one of concentric circles, with the One as the dimensionless center and Intellect and soul as the outer rings. The turning into itself of the soul became the starting point in the Academy for the study of Plato, based initially on reading *Alcibiades* I (whose Platonic authorship was not doubted in the ancient world). The latter part of the dialogue, 127e–135e, is an explanation of the Delphic maxim "Know yourself"; at 133b Socrates says that if the soul is to know itself it must look in on soul, particularly that part of soul where virtue is to be found—the seat of knowledge and thought. See further Sorabji, ed. (2004, vol. 1, 12–13 and 319–322).

1, 3 *a vision of wonderful beauty:* a vision of the beauty of the intelligible world is to be achieved, Plotinus tells us at I.6.8, 25 not by looking at beautiful objects, but by closing the eyes and adopting a different mode of seeing, an inner sight: "Return into yourself and look"

(I.6.9, 8)—the beauty that Diotima urges Socrates to pursue in *Symposium* (210a–212a).

1, 3 *I am part of the nobler realm:* the nobler realm is the intelligible world that consists of intellection and the objects of intellection, the Forms. By entering this world Plotinus becomes intellection, *at one with the divine.* (See VI.9.3, 21 quoted in the Introduction, 17.) The closer he approaches the center, the One, the more he is assimilated to Intellect, whose life is one of pure activity (= actuality).

The background is Aristotelian. First, in *Metaphysics* Lambda Aristotle characterized his god (the unmoved mover) as pure actuality; this actuality consists in intellection—intellection of intellection (*noêsis noêseôs* 1074b34), since where intellection is fully actualized its object is itself (cf. Aristotle *De Anima* 430a3ff). Secondly, divine intellection is distinguished from human intellection in that the former, containing all the forms within itself, being the perfect knower, needing nothing beside itself, is fully actualized, while the latter has potentiality for change. Here in IV.8 Plotinus envisages his own intellection as becoming at one with the divine and thereby fully actualized. Thirdly, we need to be aware of the discussion of potentiality and actuality at *DA* 2.5. Aristotle, talking about perception, takes as his analogy knowledge and says that there are two senses in which a man may be said to be potentially knowledgeable. As a member of humankind any child at birth has the capacity for acquiring knowledge; after a period of education he will have acquired knowledge; and then if he so chooses he may exercise this knowledge. These three states represent first potentiality, second potentiality = first actuality, and second actuality respectively. When he is exercising his knowledge he can be said to be most actually knowledgeable. Here Plotinus is describing his achievement of second actuality. Fourth, Plotinus adds a further refinement whereby he propounds a double activity theory. He illustrates this at V.1.3, 9ff., where he explains that just as fire has one activity within itself, heat, and one that it transmits outside itself so that objects external to it become heated, so Intellect has intellection both within itself, which is its perfected life and activity, and going out from itself; soul, in turning to its prior, receives this intellection, which becomes its perfected activity. So this is the life of perfect activity that Plotinus has achieved. He has turned inwards to be at one with Intellect and so has attained the *life of perfect activity.* See further Lloyd (1968, 140–147) and Atkinson (1985, 56–57).

1, 6 *above all the rest of the intelligible world . . . at rest in the divine:* for Aristotle potentiality implies movement and change (*kinêsis*); once the potential has been actualized, then change and movement cease and rest (*stasis*) is achieved. So once the potential for intellection has been actualized then there is rest. In this case we are asked to visualize the soul as having completed the ascent and risen above the rest of the intelligible world—the imagery of *Republic*, *Symposium* and *Phaedrus*—and so *come to rest in the divine.*

1, 8 *from intellection to discursive reasoning:* See Introduction, 24–25. At the moment of becoming at one with the divine Plotinus enjoys the activity that Intellect enjoys; but thereafter, as his descent begins, his thinking becomes increasingly discursive and pluralized. To begin with it can engage with the contents of the intelligible world, like the philosopher-king in *Republic* as he revisits the propositions of dialectic on his return journey, propositions now confirmed as truths. Thereafter he becomes increasingly embroiled in the sensible world where, of course, discursive thinking and calculation have a part to play.

It should be noted that in all this it is the reasoning faculty of the human soul that is involved, although the *Phaedrus* myth might suggest that the other faculties of the soul tag along too, so to speak. It is interesting to note that Eudorus (see Introduction, 37) understood the phrase [assimilation to god] *kata to dunaton* at *Theaetetus* 176b differently from most Platonists. They saw it as meaning "as far as is possible [for a human]," whereas

Eudorus saw it as referring to the part of the soul "with the potential," viz., to become actualized intellect. See Dillon (1977, 123). In Plotinus' case it would seem that the limitation implied is one of duration or of intensity; god enjoys everlasting and pure intellection, Plotinus only for a time (although, as we shall see, he expresses a different view in chapter 8).

1, 9 *how on earth:* The Greek interrogative adverbs *pôs* and *hopôs* used here have a wide range of application, from meaning "in what manner" to "for what reason." At this stage the argument does not require any narrowing of the scope.

1, 10 *it has been revealed to be what it is in itself:* The true nature of the soul has been revealed by its ascent as something divine, despite its association with the body. As long as the argument is confined to the soul of the person while he is alive as a compound of body and soul, is still e.g., Plotinus or Socrates, it is perhaps best to consider that the lower parts of the soul remain dormant while the rational part, the true soul, soars aloft. Plotinus does not make it entirely clear whether he believed in the survival of the lower parts of the soul after the death of the individual—he touches on the subject at IV.7.14; nor can he rely on the testimony of Plato himself, who is equally equivocal on the subject.

The medieval Arabic paraphrase of this treatise reads: "Wonderful it is too how I have seen my soul *filled with light, while she was still in my body*" (trans. G. Lewis; the italics correspond to words in Plotinus' text; "*although filled with light*" is an unusual translation of *ephanê*, which I have translated as "*it has been revealed*").

Lines 11–23

Plotinus is not averse to appealing to ancient authorities, especially those who could be seen to have influenced Plato, although he rarely mentions them by name, preferring to refer to them as "the ancients." But he generally pays scant attention to them; nor are they mentioned by Porphyry as among Plotinus' sources. Armstrong (Loeb, vol. 4, 398) commenting on this passage says: "As always he [Plotinus] spends little time in considering the Presocratics and does not seem to find them very helpful." Stamatellos (2007) attempts to establish the Presocratics as important sources for Plotinus' thought, especially in this treatise. Plotinus does indeed mention Heraclitus twice and Empedocles three times by name in this treatise. Although he dismisses them, there must have been something in what they (and the Pythagoreans) said that aroused his interest. Bréhier (1956, 212) refers to *Gorgias* 492e–493b, where Plato, discussing the presence of soul in body, quotes a line of Euripides "Who knows if life be death or death be life?" as being inspired by Heraclitus, and follows with a reference to an opinion of a sage "that the body is a tomb"—the sage being a Sicilian or an Italian, possibly Empedocles.

1, 11 *Heraclitus:* our knowledge of Heraclitus is fragmentary and controversial. Plotinus here appears to be quoting—perhaps from memory and so not necessarily accurately—four apothegms, which the present context suggests that he is taking as referring to the soul, although the original scope may have been wider. *Dicta Sapientis Graeci* on 5.6 says: "Heraclitus said 'When I erred I descended to this world in order to rest, and through it I came into greater fatigue and weariness.'"

1, 12 *necessary changes between opposites:* this appears to pick up fr. B90 "all things are a repayment for fire, and fire for all things, just like goods for gold and gold for goods." The traditional interpretation of this (but see Kahn 1979, 132–153) is that Heraclitus is describing the cosmic interchange of elements in which fire dominates. Although it is not clear that Heraclitus himself identified soul with fire, it would seem that Plotinus here is at least entertaining the possibility. Taken with the next phrase *the way up is the way down*—given a similar assumption on the part of Plotinus—then he is suggesting that Heraclitus is saying that the ascent and descent of the soul are part of a necessary cyclic exchange; what goes up must come down. Similarly with the subsequent phrases (for which the only known testimony is this passage of Plotinus) *what changes is at repose* and *weariness is to toil and to be making a start at the same thing*. There is much scholarly disagreement on the translation of the latter, particularly on the meaning of the verb *arkhesthai* which can mean variously "to make a start," "to rule" or "to be ruled," and of the case and gender of *tois autois (the same)*. If we adopt a psychological reading of these phrases, then the meaning could be that there is a constant interchange for the soul between repose and weariness. Inge (1948, vol. 2, 256) says: "Heraclitus tells us that the pendulum of life swings necessarily between two contraries, that the way up is the way down, and that change is good in itself, bringing relief from ennui." Iamblichus, a pupil of Porphyry (*De Anima* §26: 378 Finamore-Dillon) says, with his eye on this passage of Plotinus: "To persist in the same situation is restlessness, while to change brings repose"—which matches Heraclitus' often paradoxical mode of expression. Iamblichus and Aeneas Gazaeus are both cited by HS_2 *ad loc.* as taking these words of Plotinus in a psychological context, as does the medieval Arabic paraphrase. The soul feels weariness when it is in the intelligible world, and it is this ennui that causes it to "fall."

1, 16 *his argument:* the Greek word is *logos* and it may be that Plotinus is indulging in some wordplay. What is generally agreed to be the opening phrase of Heraclitus' work is more than ambiguous: "Although this *logos* abides for ever men fail to understand it," where *logos* can mean either "my account" or "the underlying principle of the cosmos." So Plotinus' *double-entendre* would amount to "Heraclitus fails to give a proper account" and "Heraclitus fails to explain his universal law."

1, 17 *search within himself:* this phrase recalls with Heraclitus fr. 116: "All men should seek to know themselves," fr. 101: "I went in search of myself," and fr. 115: "The *logos* of the soul is fathomless."

See further Stamatellos (2007, 158–166).

1, 17 *Empedocles too:* The quotation is from fr. 115, a passage in total of 14 lines of hexameter verse in which Empedocles tells that there is an oracle of Necessity requiring *daimones* that have sinned to enter into a cycle of 30,000 years of birth and rebirth into all variety of living creatures. Empedocles ends by saying that he is one of those sinners and is now *an exile from the divine, obedient to maddened strife.* This is not the place to review the extended scholarly debate (well summarized by Warren [2007, ch. 8, especially 146–152]). It is sufficient to say that Plotinus was perhaps initially attracted by two features of Empedocles' account, first the cyclic nature of the soul's passage in and out of the body (he seems to equate "soul" with *daimôn*) and secondly the enduring identity of that soul throughout the 30,000 years, even if not as a nameable individual or as a human being. But the fact that Empedocles sees the descent into the body exclusively as a punishment for sin does not suit Plotinus. This saying of Empedocles is quoted again at IV.8.5, 5 with the paraphrase of *Dicta Sapientis Graeci:* "Empedocles said 'I entered this world as a fugitive from the wrath of God Almighty because I erred and feared punishment, and now I have entered that which I had been fearing.'"

1, 19 *exile from the divine:* The Greek word for exile is *phugas* and contrasts with Plotinus' use of *phugê* (escape) e.g., at VI.9.11, 51 "the escape of the solitary to the solitary" to echo Plato *Theaetetus* 176ab: "So we should try to escape as quickly as possible from this to that world; escape is assimilation to god as far as is possible."

1, 20 *obedient to maddened strife:* This seems to refer to the rule of Strife in Empedocles' cosmogony, and is given here as a reason for the soul's sinfulness; as Warren (2007, 148) puts it: "This would assign an ethical dimension to Love and Strife, since Love would be associated with harmony and proper conduct, and Strife with transgression and disorder."

1, 21 *Pythagoras and his followers:* Plotinus has little general regard for Pythagoras, whom he attacks in IV.7.8[4] for his theory that the soul is an attunement. Here he appears to be including Pythagoras "*and his followers*" with Empedocles as believers in the transmigration of souls, which does not match the attunement theory. See Barnes (1982, 103–120). Just what Plotinus means by *his followers* is equally unclear, but it is clear that the ancients accepted many so-called Pythagorean sources now shown to be spurious. See Thesleff (1965, *passim*) and Fleet (1995, 88–89).

1, 21 *spoke in riddles:* the Greek verb *ainittesthai* is according to Atkinson (1995, 179) "one of the technical terms of allegorical writing. Plotinus commonly uses the word of the riddling language of myth and mystery religions."

1, 23 *he writes in verse:* Empedocles, together with Hesiod (fl. c. 700 BCE) and Parmenides (c. 515–450 BCE) represent the early Greek tradition of instructional (didactic) poetry. It is thought that (hexameter) verse was a more memorable medium of instruction in a period before widespread literacy, although that cannot have been the sole motive for Empedocles' and Parmenides' employing it, since their predecessor Heraclitus, *inter alios*, was already writing sophisticated prose. So perhaps Empedocles and Parmenides felt that verse gave added authority to their words—or rather the words of the divine authority they both appealed to.

Lines 23–41

The rest of the chapter is devoted to Plato. Plotinus starts by referring to doctrines of Plato that suggest that the sensible world is an undesirable region (lines 28–41); he then turns to *Timaeus*, which is a work of a more optimistic tone, not only when talking about the operations of the soul of the cosmos but also those of individual souls. Plotinus is setting the agenda for the ensuing discussion.

1, 29 *association of the soul with the body:* At *Phaedo* 67a Socrates says that we can only aspire to pure knowledge during our earthly lifetime "if we have, as far as possible, no intercourse or association with the body."

1, 30 *is in fetters:* At *Phaedo* 67d Plato in urging us to attain purification says that we should withdraw our soul from contact with the body, as far as possible, and allow it to live "alone, by itself, freed from the fetters of the body" (on the religious connotations of purification of the soul, see Fleet [1995, 139–140]); the prisoners in the Cave in *Republic* are fettered (see Introduction, 19–21); at *Cratylus* 400c, where the derivation of the word *sôma* (body) is being discussed, one suggestion from the Orphics is that the soul is encased in the body as if it were in a prisonlike enclosure; and, of course, Socrates was in prison from his trial until his death in

399 BCE, and a constant theme in *Phaedo* is that his death will be a release.

1, 31 *is entombed in the body:* At *Gorgias* 493a Socrates says that he has heard from some clever man that "we are now dead, and the body is our tomb *(sôma)*"; Sextus Empiricus at *Outlines of Pyrrhonism* 3.230 reports Heraclitus as saying: "When we are alive our souls are dead and buried within us," which may be a paraphrase of fr. 62: "Mortals are immortal, immortals mortal, living their deaths and dying their lives" with the addition of the verb *tethaphthai* (are buried).

1, 31 *the secret saying:* this is a quotation from *Phaedo* 62b, where Socrates, talking about suicide, says: "The secret saying about them which claims that we humans are under surveillance and that we should not release ourselves or even desert from it seems to me to be a great saying and one hard to understand"; Plotinus seems to be understanding the word *phroura* as denoting some sort of imprisonment, although the context of *Phaedo* suggests that the secret saying referred to here is some Orphic-Pythagorean belief that the human soul is "on guard duty" in the body—Burnet (1911, on 62b3) quotes passages from Cicero and the Stoics that support this military interpretation as well as other passages from Greek authors that state, by contrast, that it was a Pythagorean doctrine that the body is the prison-house of the soul. Plotinus is clearly adopting this latter interpretation here. There are several other allusions in Plato's dialogues to the body as a prison, e.g., *Phaedo* 82de, *Timaeus* 44b.

1, 33 *the Cave . . . a release from its fetters . . . an ascent:* these phrases all refer to the ascent from the Cave described in *Republic* (see Introduction, 19–21).

1, 33 *Empedocles:* this is a brief quotation from Empedocles (fr. 120) found in Porphyry's *On the Cavern of the Nymphs*, an allegorizing interpretation of the story in Homer *Odyssey* 5, which reads: "We entered this roofed cavern" and seems to tell of the descent into earthly existence of fallen *daimones*—at least that is Plotinus' interpretation. See above on 1.17.

1, 37 *loss of wings . . . cycles which return the soul . . . judgments . . . casting of lots:* See Introduction, 25–28. The *judgment (krisis)* of souls is referred to at *Phaedrus* 249a, where we are told that souls of men other than successful philosophers and philosophic lovers, who regain their wings after the third 1,000 year *cycle*, receive *judgment* at the end of their first life, some of whom are despatched to the Underworld for correction while others proceed to a part of the Heavens to live in the manner that they deserve because of the merits of their earthly life. At the end of each 1,000 years they come to draw *lots* for their next earthly life. (The word *cycle* is also used at 247d to describe the procession of the gods around the circuit of the cosmos, but that is not the cycle Plotinus is referring to here.) The *judgment* of mortals after death is found in several places in Plato, e.g., *Phaedo* 107d, *Gorgias* 523b, but the idea is certainly not confined to Platonism.

1, 38 *judgments . . . casting of lots . . .fortune . . . necessity:* All these terms are found in *Republic* 10 in the passage known as The Myth of Er, which, as Guthrie (1975, 557) says "is a grand apocalypse relating the soul and its fate to the structure and processes of the whole cosmic order" as the conclusion of *Republic.* Er, a fictitious Pamphylian, has been supposedly killed in battle and his body is awaiting cremation, although not at all decomposed (he eventually is resuscitated). His soul is miraculously taken to the Underworld where he sees the souls of men being judged and despatched either to the Underworld or to the Heavens for a *cycle* of 1,000 years before returning to draw lots for their next life. He sees an elaborate vision of "the spindle of *Necessity,*" which is being turned by the three Fates, the daughters of *Necessity;* one of these, Lachesis, distributes *lots* to the waiting souls to determine the order in which they are to choose their next life—which is subject to "the *luck* of the draw." There is however a note of optimism in that the lives chosen are not all unhappy; it is the general case that those who have suffered in the Underworld have the sense to choose a better life than many of those who come from their period in the Heavens. So these references lead Plotinus to the final part of the chapter where a more optimistic note is sounded.

Lines 41–50

1, 41 *Timaeus:* In lines 41–50 Plotinus summarizes some points in *Timaeus* that appear to be in conflict with those that he has just noted in other dialogues, where Plato is *censuring the approach of soul to body. Timaeus* was an important work for Plotinus and the Neoplatonists who followed him. It was written towards the end of Plato's life and was published around 350 BCE as part of an unfinished trilogy that was to comprise *Timaeus*, *Critias* and *Hermocrates.* In it the (probably fictitious) Timaeus of Locri in southern Italy is invited to join the discussion by giving his account of the origin of the cosmos. Timaeus is supposed by some to be a Pythagorean so that his views are not necessarily those of Plato himself. But this was not the understanding of Plotinus, and I follow him in assuming that the account we are given is Platonic, and that in reality the speaker is Plato. See Wilberding (2006, 69), who quotes a single instance in Plotinus (II.1.6, 6–8) where a distinction is made between Timaeus and Plato. In *Timaeus* we are given a creation myth on the grounds that no incontrovertible account of the cosmos and its creation can be given, but only a "likely" one. It should be noted that Plotinus does not subscribe to the view that *Timaeus* describes a process that took place at a particular time; rather, as he makes clear at III.7.6, 50, "the cosmos did not have a beginning in time"; rather the process of creation is an eternal process of change.

He starts by drawing a distinction familiar to readers of Plato between the intelligible world and the sensible world (this latter being the cosmos) and establishes a causal link between them. Just as in the production of any artefact the good craftsman (demiurge) will look to an intelligible pattern and not to a sensible, and therefore unreliable, copy, so too the demiurge of the cosmos; "If this cosmos is beautiful *(kalos)* and *its maker is good (agathos)*, he must have looked to what is eternal . . . for the cosmos is the best of the things that have come to be, and the craftsman is the best of all causes" (29aff.)—in the words of Cornford (1937, 26) he is "a perpetual sustaining cause." The eternal pattern is identified as the Ideal Living Creature—a generic Form containing the specific Forms of all living creatures, so that the cosmos is a living creature. At 29e Plato states the aims of the demiurge: "He was good . . . and he wanted everything to be as like himself as possible." Seeing that intelligent beings are superior to non-intelligent entities, and that intelligence can be present only in soul, "this cosmos was in truth created as an *ensouled intelligent* creature because of the foresight of the god."

At 34a he says, of the material body of the cosmos, that it is divine and that at its center the god set a soul that extended throughout its mass and enclosed it all round, and at 34b he says: "For all these reasons he made it a *blessed god*." So for Plotinus the arrival of the soul of the cosmos in the body of the cosmos is blessed and divine. There is certainly some anti-Gnostic polemic hidden in these words; Plotinus devotes much energy in countering the Gnostics within his own circle; for example Porphyry entitles II.9 "Against the Gnostics," and it is perhaps part of a longer treatise subsequently divided by Porphyry. One Gnostic doctrine that Plotinus vehemently opposes is that the demiurge in ignorance had created a flawed cosmos; he lacked the foresight of Plato's demiurge.

He then proceeds briefly to account for the arrival of individual souls in bodies. One important feature of *Timaeus* that Plotinus does not allude to here is that the demiurge was obliged to work with pre-existing chaotic unruly materials. Sedley (2007, 113–127) argues persuasively as against Cornford (1937, 161–177) that the demiurge had complete control over his materials so that indeed the cosmos is perfect, and that the arrival of both the cosmic and the individual soul leads to its perfection. The overall aim of the demiurge is the benefit of human souls, which cannot be achieved without pain. But the question of why human souls err is not addressed at this point in the treatise. All Plotinus tells us is that individual souls contribute to the perfection of the cosmos, since otherwise the Ideal Living Creature would not be properly imaged in the cosmos. Nor does Plotinus here mention that the demiurge, in Plato's account, leaves the inculcation of the lower parts of the human soul to the lesser gods that he himself has created, confining his own role to that of implanting the rational part of the soul into humans.

1, 48 *so that the All might be perfected:* the Greek word for "perfected" is *teleos*, which can also be translated as "complete." At 30d Plato says: "Because the god wished to make it as similar as possible to the intelligible being which is most beautiful and complete in every respect, he made it a single visible living creature containing within itself all the living creatures which are of its own nature." Anything short of that would result in the cosmos' being incomplete or imperfect.

Chapter 2

Having made the distinction between the soul of the cosmos and individual souls, Plotinus turns to consider the differences and similarities a little more closely, with regard to their descent (or arrival) into bodies. He does not here demythologize *Timaeus*, but elsewhere, e.g., V.1.6–7, his account is: the One *(to hen)*, in its sheer one-ness, overflows (the Greek verb is *ekrein* = the Latin *emanare*, hence the English term "emanation"); the as yet undefined overflow turns back *(epistrephetai)* to contemplate its source and in so doing gains definition as Intellect *(Nous);* the overflow of this contemplation of its prior likewise gains definition as Soul *(psukhê);* the overflow of Soul's contemplation of its prior is the raw material of the cosmos, but unlike the One and Intellect, which take no notice of their emanations (Intellect and Soul), Soul is concerned with the ordering of what comes after it, and the result is organized matter, the cosmos. But increasing separation from the One involves increasing pluralization and so "soul as a whole" *(pasa psukhê)* becomes pluralized into the soul of the cosmos and individual souls, which are species of soul like elder and younger sisters. Individual souls can be embodied in either the planets and stars, or in individual animals, especially humans; Plotinus does not in this treatise (IV.8) concern himself with the souls of animals and plants. But Soul is an organic whole and these differences within it mirror the differences within a generic Form, its species and its instantiations. O'Meara (1993, 67) summarizes: "The differences between soul, world soul (the soul of the cosmos) and individual souls make best sense in relation to differences in their relationship to body; body is what produces the distinction between souls. However Plotinus rejects this; he claims that souls are different from each other independently of, and prior to, their presence in bodies, as part of their constitution as an expression of divine intellect." Whereas the association of the soul of the cosmos with the material cosmos, since the cosmos as a whole is perfect, is unproblematic—as is the association of the souls of the planets and stars with their bodies—the association of individual human souls with bodies that are not perfect is problematic. It is this descent into a pluralized and imperfect world that is at the root of Plotinus' inquiry. Even so we should not lose sight of the fact that the human soul is not only embodied in this way, but also remains in part in the intelligible world. (See further Gerson [1994, 63–64] and Blumenthal [1971] for different views; both of them offer a broad range of passages from various of Plotinus' treatises, but neither pays much attention to Plato, especially *Timaeus*.)

Lines 1–14

In these lines Plotinus deals with the relation of soul to material body by posing a series of questions, asking whether the cosmos was brought into being "correctly" *(orthôs)* by its maker so as to avoid the contamination experienced by individual souls.

2, 3 *soul in general:* The original question posed at the start of chapter 1 was about the individual soul, but in order to answer that question we must look wider and consider the nature of "soul in general," "soul as a whole."

2, 3 *to associate with body:* The Greek verb for "to associate" is *koinônein*, a word frequently used by Plato to indicate the relationship between intelligible and sensible, e.g., at *Phaedo* 100d, where it denotes the association between (material) subject and (immaterial) predicate or quality; Plotinus too used it e.g., at I.8.14, 52 to indicate the relationship between soul and matter. The nature of such a relationship was questioned by Plato himself at *Parmenides* 128eff. The doctrine of emanation was Plotinus' answer (see O'Meara [1993, ch. 2]).

2, 5 *willingly or under compulsion or in some other way:* Plotinus gives notice of a problem that he himself found puzzling throughout his life. This is because Plato himself does not give a clear answer, as Plotinus hints at 1.27: ". . . .he does not always speak with sufficient consistency for us to make out his intentions with any ease." Generally speaking, Plotinus is equivocal on the nature of the descent of human souls. At times he suggests that the soul's descent is voluntary, at others involuntary. Dodds (1965, 24–26) thinks that Plotinus changed his mind after his break with the Gnostics and moved from viewing the descent as voluntary to seeing it as involuntary. O'Brien (1977) suggests that the two terms need not be mutually exclusive; this is borne out by IV.3.13, 17 "Souls go down neither voluntarily nor because they are sent; at least, such volition is not like a choice, but like a natural jump such as the urge for sexual intercourse or for noble action." Other passages in Plotinus are inconclusive and it is perhaps less profitable to seek for a single definite doctrine than to attend to the discussion in this treatise. Atkinson (1983, 6) concludes: "I am not convinced that Plotinus' views of the awkward problem of the descent of the soul ever showed any real development." Plotinus deals more fully with this issue in chapter 5.

There are several places where Plato talks about the descent of soul, particularly the descent of the individual soul either during the person's lifetime or between lives. He chooses to describe it by means of myth, for example in *Phaedrus* where the chariot of the soul is dragged off course by the appetitive horse—which would suggest a willing descent; or in *Republic* where the philosopher king is required to return to the cave after his sojourn in the realms of intellect—which would suggest a descent under compulsion; or in the Myth of Er in *Republic* and in the myth in *Gorgias* where souls are despatched to a new life by divine powers but with some choice over their new life—which would suggest a mixture of willingness and compulsion.

But it is in *Timaeus* that Plato gives his most sustained account, an account that deals with the soul of the cosmos, the souls of stars and planets, and individual human souls.

2, 7 *for since they govern inferior bodies:* From this point as far as line 19 *(for nothing leaves or is added)* Plotinus offers a contrast. On the one hand the cosmos, which we might suppose to be all that there is, is presented as the perfect expression of the creativity of the demiurge; it is the complete image of the Ideal Living Creature, and the materials that comprise the cosmos are the consequence of the turning of Soul to contemplate its prior, Intellect, and the product is the product of reason. But if this were the whole story we would be left with a cosmos like that of Parmenides' One in which there is no differentiation, imperfection, plurality or change possible. Plato, however, is not the out-and-out rationalist that Parmenides is; he is prepared to accept not only the intelligible world of real being *(ontôs on)* but also the sketchy being "of a sort" of the sensible world *(onta pôs)* and, beyond that acceptance, to seek a causal and ontological link between the two worlds. In this he is followed by Plotinus, and although Plotinus chooses to express his views in figurative language rather than myth, *Timaeus* remains for him a seminal work.

Plotinus has talked about body in general in the second sentence of this chapter ("How on earth is it in the nature of soul to associate with body?"). He now deals with the bodies of individuals that need the controlling force of soul to prevent their dissolution. Therein lies their inferiority—the ensouled is always superior to the unensouled.

2, 10 *in the All all bodies:* Either Plotinus is explaining the statement "each body would be scattered, swept away to its proper place" by appealing to the universal principle that all things, primarily the four elements of which the individual body is composed, find their natural place after the dissolution of the body. Or else he is pointing a contrast between individual human bodies, which are subject to dissolution, and cosmic bodies. The latter fall under two headings: (a) the heavenly bodies that enjoy everlasting stability (cf. II.1.5), and (b) the four elemental bodies, each of which has its *proper place* determined by its relative density, with fire the most rarified, air next, water next and earth the densest. The cosmos is a sphere and the four primary bodies would most naturally form four concentric spheres, with earth at the centre and fire at the perimeter, since the rotation of the cosmos exerts both a centrifugal and a centripetal force. Cf. Simplicius *On Aristotle's Physics* 2.263, 26–29 and 287, 30 where he is discussing Aristotle's definition of nature as "having an internal principle of motion and rest," and quotes *de Caelo (On the Heavens)* 284b33: "In none of the un-ensouled beings can we see the origin of the source of movement. For some are not moved at all, others are moved but not similarly from every side—for example fire which is only moved upwards, and earth which is moved towards the centre." That is their nature. Here Plotinus is asserting that at the macrocosmic level there is an underlying stability and equilibrium, and that the soul of the cosmos is not concerned with what occurs at a lower microcosmic level.

But the concern of individual souls of humans is with the individual bodies that do not naturally enjoy such stability and equilibrium. They are embroiled in the sensible world, a pluralized world where the struggle between reason and necessity is constantly raging. The bodies into which individual souls are implanted are compounds of the four elements and need to be constantly controlled *("need much painstaking foresight")* to preserve their compound nature and avoid disintegration into separate elements, which naturally seek their proper place in the cosmos. There is an ambiguity in the way that Plotinus uses the term "body"; on the one hand it denotes the four primary bodies, fire, air, water and earth; on the other it denotes the human body which is a compound of the four primary bodies. When he says *each body* he is referring to the human body, so that when it is *scattered, swept away to its proper place* he means that it is first broken down into its constituent primary bodies, and these then join their like in the cosmos at large (Armstrong translates "as otherwise each [element of the individual bodies] would be dispersed and carried to its appropriate place"). This would be true of any ensouled creature such as an animal or plant—the soul as life principle is what holds it together. Disintegration ensues when the soul can no longer perform the task. Non-ensouled things such as stones or flames are under the control of the soul of the cosmos.

Plotinus would certainly deny that there is any positive evil force at play in the cosmos—that would be a tenet of the Gnosticism that he eschewed. Rather evil is seen as an absence of good—the One is the Good—and distance from the One is distance from the Good, although

Plotinus exempts the whole of the intelligible world, including the higher reaches of soul. Evil is no more than a necessary product of emanation at the level of the sensible world. And matter is evil in this restricted sense. This is broadly the conclusion reached in a late treatise, I [51].8. See further note on 5, 28.

2, 12 *alien forces:* The human being, the conjoint of soul and body, is beset by forces that, unless checked, cause disruption and the dispersal of its elements. This can happen at any time during one's lifetime. As soon as the child is born it is subject to the onslaught of alien forces from outside itself, something that the heavenly bodies and the body of the cosmos do not have to deal with. At *Timaeus* 42eff. we are told that the lesser gods, following the instructions of their father (the demiurge) "having taken an immortal principle of a mortal creature . . . borrowed portions of fire, earth, water and air from the cosmos . . . and enclosed the circuits of the immortal soul within the ebb and flow of the body." These infant creatures were thrown back and to by the six irrational motions (up, down, to, fro, to this side, to that side) and buffeted by the assault of elements from outside; these are the *alien forces.* As the other irrational parts of the soul were later added and they received correct nurture and education, they learned to survive the onslaught. There is a constant depletion and replenishment of the elements during one's lifetime; 81a "what surrounds us from outside is always dissolving and dispersing our substance distributing each to its like," but there is constant replenishment. When the replenishment ceases to keep pace with the depletion, the bonds holding the body together are weakened, and so old age and eventually death ensues, which is natural and nothing unpleasant. But death by disease or violence is unnatural and unpleasant, and these are what we seek to avoid. Disease can be predominantly bodily, when there is an unnatural prevalence or deficiency of any one or more elements. Or else it can be predominantly psychic, when bodily concerns are allowed to take precedence. So *bodies need much painstaking foresight* if we are to live a good life; "healthy mind in healthy body." At 87b–89d Plato gives a prescription for the proper care of the body. But paramount is the care of the soul, by which we can "as far as is possible for a human partake of immortality," 90b.

Lines 14–19

In these lines Plotinus asserts that the cosmos is perfect and self-sufficient, and so applies no *alien forces* to the soul of the cosmos.

2, 14 *But the cosmos:* By contrast the cosmos is perfect, as we have seen, and its soul has none of these worries. Unlike human souls, which have in addition to the immortal rational part the two lower irrational parts (familiar from *Republic* and *Phaedrus*), the appetitive and the spirited, the soul of the cosmos is entirely rational. So it has no appetites and cannot be affected (*Ennead* III.6 is entitled *On the Impassivity of the Bodiless*, and sets out to show that soul *qua* soul cannot suffer any affections; see Fleet [1995]). The two lower parts are added to human souls by the lesser gods. The cosmos is described by Plato at *Timaeus* 33b–34a in terms of its perfection and self-sufficiency.

2, 18 *nothing leaves or is added:* this phrase is quoted from *Timaeus* 33c, in a passage where Plato gives a description of the cosmos. The cosmos is the complete and perfect copy of the Ideal Living Creature, and as such it can have no need of anything else—in fact there is nothing else beside it. See Wilberding (2006, 106–108) for a list of references outside Plato for the idea that the cosmos is self-sufficient, especially Aristotle *de Philosophia* fr.19 (= Philo *de Aeternitate Mundi* 21): "If the universe perishes, it must be the case that it will perish either by one of the powers external to it or from one of the powers in itself. But each of these cases is impossible: For there is nothing outside the universe as everything has contributed to its completeness. Therefore in this way it will be one and a whole and ageless"; and Chrysippus SVF 2.604: "The cosmos alone is said to be sufficient because it alone contains in itself all things that it requires; further, it is nourished and grows from itself when the other parts change into one another."

Lines 19–26

Plotinus now gives an optimistic view of the individual soul when it is at its best, when it withdraws from the body and joins the soul of the cosmos in providential care for the cosmos.

2, 19 *That is why Plato says:* The quotation *[itself reaches perfection] journeying on high and organising the whole cosmos* is from *Phaedrus* 246c, where the full sentence is: "Being perfect and winged it journeys on high and organizes the whole cosmos." It refers to the myth of the charioteer (see Introduction, 25–28), but is compatible with many other passages in Plato, e.g., the journey of Socrates with Diotima in *Symposium*, and the instruction given by the demiurge to the lesser gods to keep a constant watch on human souls.

2, 21 *when it withdraws:* When it "assimilates to god."

2, 24 *for it is no way an evil:* At *Phaedrus* 246b Plato says: "Soul as a whole has care of all that is non-ensouled," which is a principle that permeates *Timaeus* and much else of Plato's work. Plotinus seeks to draw a line between the care that preserves the integrity of the soul of the carer—the care shown to an inferior by the soul of the cosmos, by the lesser gods and by human souls at their best—and care that compromises the integrity of the carer. It is this latter that makes a prison-house of the body.

Lines 26–38

Plotinus now shows in more detail how the soul of the cosmos remains uncontaminated by its association with the cosmos at large, even though displaying providential care for it.

2, 26 *for there are two sorts of caring:* We learn in *Timaeus* that in order to perfect the copy of the Ideal Living Creature, its body and all the species present in it must be brought into being. Among these are the four species of living creature—the gods of the heavens, winged creatures, aquatic creatures, and those that live on the face of the earth. The demiurge completes the body and soul of the cosmos and then the lesser gods, whom he installs in the stars and the planets together with the immortal parts of individual souls. But his creative progress halts there, and he delegates to the lesser gods the task of creating the bodies of individuals and the lower parts of the individual soul. He gives the reason for this delegation in an address to the lesser gods (*Timaeus* 41a–d): the three species of living creature yet to be made are mortal; but if the demiurge, who is divine, were to make them, they too would be immortal; so the lesser gods are to take the immortal part of the individual soul and join it together with the mortal parts of the soul and the body, and so create humankind; "Weaving the mortal to the immortal, create living creatures and give them birth; give them sustenance to make them grow, and when they perish take them back again." No other explanation is considered necessary. The demiurge is not shirking unpleasant tasks, but is by his very nature unable to fulfil them. A hierarchy has thus evolved, with the demiurge at the head acting as the eternal creative principle. After the primary organization of the cosmos and the team that is to be responsible for its continuing state he retires from the scene and we hear little of him in the later part of *Timaeus*, and the soul of the cosmos and the individual souls take up the task. It is to their functions that Plotinus now turns his attention.

He introduces a simile at line 26 drawn from the political (or possibly military) scene. This is unsurprising since, although he had little active involvement in politics himself—he had unsuccessfully proposed to the emperor Gallienus the setting up of a city of philosophers to be called Platonopolis (Porphyry *VP* 12). Plato too had more than one abortive attempt to involve himself in the politics of Sicily, and Plotinus was steeped in the political works of Plato, notably *Republic* and *Laws*. This thought, however, was already firmly established in the philosophical tradition; cf. Aristotle *Metaphysics* 1075a14ff. and Ps.-Aristotle *de Mundo* 398a6ff. The details of the simile are unproblematic.

2, 29 *which infects the doer with the nature of the operation:* This is an echo of *Phaedo* 67a: we should avoid except where absolutely necessary intercourse with the body "so that we should not be infected by its nature."

2, 32 *remaining aloof in its highest aspect:* There is no word in the Greek for *aspect*—Plotinus uses just the neuter of the word *kreittôn* (= higher, better) as a substantive, lit. "the better thing." MacKenna renders it as "phase," and Armstrong as "part." Armstrong's version is misleading in that it suggests that the soul of the cosmos has "parts" in the way that the human soul is tripartite, which is not the case. Plotinus possibly has in mind a passage at *Theaetetus* 189e and 206d, and *Sophist* 263e, where a distinction is made between discursive thought *(dianoia)* as "the conversation *(dialogos)* conducted internally by the soul with itself without speech" and discourse *(logos)* which is "the articulated outflow from the soul through the mouth." This concept is developed by the Stoics and later taken over by Plotinus as the distinction between the *logos* in conception *(logos endiathetos)* and the *logos* in expression *(logos prophorikos).* See Atkinson (1993, 59–64) for a full discussion, and cf. note on 3, 6. Another way of putting the idea is to say that the soul of the cosmos has an internal activity of its own, and a second activity, rather confusingly termed here as a "power" (*dunamis*, which in other contexts can mean "potentiality"), that it transmits to its posteriors. The soul that we are dealing with here is the soul of the cosmos, which derives from Soul the hypostasis.

2.35 *what is in its nature:* Plato describes at some length in *Timaeus* the composition and the nature of the soul of the cosmos (34b–37c). It holds a position between the eternality of the intelligible world and the transitory nature of the sensible world. Plato gives a complex description of its composition out of (a) a blend of indivisible and divisible Being, (b) indivisible and divisible Sameness and (c) indivisible and divisible Difference. The three terms Being, Sameness and Difference derive from *Sophist* where they are described as being the "three most important Forms" *(megista genê)* in which all other Forms share (along with Rest and Motion). Indivisibility is the hallmark of the contents of the intelligible world, and divisibility of the sensible world; Soul occupies an intermediate position. Cf. Proclus (5th century CE): *Commentary on the Timaeus* 2, 117: There are three orders of Being, "intelligible and ungenerated (the contents of the intelligible world); perceptible and generated things (the contents of the sensible world); and intermediate things that are intelligible and generated (Soul)"; and *ibid.*2, 147: "There is a difference between the everlastingness which is eternal and the everlastingness which is spread out along the infinity of time; and there is yet another, composed of both, such as belongs to the soul. For in its being the soul is unchangeable and eternal, but in respect of its thoughts it is in change and in time." Further at *Laws* 896a Soul is said to be "that which can set itself and other things in motion," and at 896bc the "correct, authoritative, truest and most complete statement is that soul was generated as prior to body and body second and posterior to it, with soul ruling and body by nature being ruled." Soul has cognitive powers too: Proclus 2, 298: "Since the soul consists of three parts, Being, Sameness and Difference, in a form intermediate between the indivisible and the divisible, by means of these she knows both orders of things . . . for all knowing is accomplished by means of likeness between the knower and the known" (Cornford 1937, 94). So Plotinus is saying that although it is in the nature of the soul of the cosmos to be directed both upwards and downwards, its nature cannot be affected by this latter activity.

Lines 38–53

Plotinus turns now to consider the souls of the stars, which we are told were created by the demiurge and assigned to the stars and planets. They have a nature akin to that of the soul of the cosmos. Just as the soul of the cosmos causes axial rotation in the cosmos at large, so they cause the axial rotation of the individual stars and planets—which are also carried round on the periphery of the cosmos by its axial rotation. *Laws* 898e offers three different ways in which the souls of stars might move their bodies. They too remain aloof from but aware of the movement and changes in the sensible world. The words of Plato alluded to in *the souls of the stars bear the same relation to their bodies . . . into the circles of the soul* are to be found at *Timaeus* 38c, where the reference is to the seven planets (often loosely termed "stars") that "are stationed in the orbits along which the revolution of the Different moved . . . to determine and preserve the measures of time." They are all composed mainly of fire as is appropriate for them in their position on the outer rim of the heavens. The further description at 40ab of the nature of not only the planets (including earth) but also the fixed stars fits with what Plotinus says here. Plato's summary at 40b is: "In this way the fixed stars were created, being divine living creatures, everlasting, abiding always and revolving in the same place; and those that turn, "wandering" in that sense, have been created in the manner described." (The Greek word *planêtês* means "wanderer.") So apart from being guardians of time because of their "wanderings" the planets do not differ from the fixed stars. And in their totality they bear the same relation to their bodies as does the soul of the cosmos to its body.

2, 44 *it inhibits intellection:* At *Phaedo* 65ab Socrates says that since the bodily senses, especially sight and hearing, do not give accurate information, we are inhibited by our bodies from gaining any true knowledge *(phronêsis)*, which can only be gained when we are free of the distractions of the senses such as *pains* and *pleasures:* and at 66c he says that the body fills us with sexual passions, *appetites*, fears and all sorts of fancies and nonsense, so that we lose our sight of the truth.

2, 46 *sunk inside the body* This picks up line 8: *they were bound to sink deep inside them.*

2, 49 *this soul:* The soul of the cosmos, whose *blessed better vision* is its contemplation of Intellect. As we have seen (lines 30–33) the soul of the cosmos is directed, in its higher aspect, upwards. It need have no apprehensions about its body, which is perfect, needing nothing. The *power that remains uninvolved* is the power that it transmits into the world. What Plotinus does not add here is that the soul of the cosmos and the souls of the stars are uniate in that they are entirely immortal and rational, whereas the souls of individual humans have been given the two mortal irrational parts by the lesser gods in addition to the immortal part bestowed by the demiurge, and are thus tripartite.

Chapter 3

Lines 1–6

BEFORE FINALLY TURNING to the main topic of the treatise, the descent of the individual human soul into bodies, Plotinus draws distinctions between it and Intellect (as a whole and as individual intellects), which could be also said to descend, but in a different manner.

3, 1 *is said to suffer:* Plotinus seems to be distancing himself from the view that the soul can be affected, by using the words *is said to be.* The term *suffer harmful affections (kakopathein)* is used on only one other occasion by Plotinus, at III.2.2, 41, where he says that the soul of the cosmos "suffers no harmful affections." He devotes the first five chapters of his treatise III.6 to show that the individual soul can suffer affections, but in only a very restricted sense. (See Fleet [1995, xix]: "Our common experience, reflected in the way that we talk, might suggest that the individual soul, which is most closely linked to the body, in some way shares the affections of the body; but to admit that the soul is affected in the same way as the body would be also to admit its destructibility. Plotinus must therefore show that the soul is not liable to affection in this way.") The verb *kakopathein* and its cognates are used widely by Greek authors, e.g., Thucydides and Xenophon, in a non-technical sense. But Plotinus may be using it here in a more technical sense in contrast to the Stoic term *eupatheia* ("good affections") which is attested by Diogenes Laertius (7.16 = SVF 3.431) and Plutarch (*de Virtute Morali* 449b). (See LS 65F.) James Warren (in conversation) suggests that Plotinus might be using the verb *kakopathein* here to avoid confusion with the Stoic term *pathos*, which for them signifies an irrational feeling, whereas for Plotinus it has a more neutral connotation, "affection."

3, 2 *follies, desires, fears:* A repeat of some of the affections listed in chapter 2, 44ff.

3, 4 *fetter, tomb, cave and cavern:* A repeat of the items listed at chapter 1, 30ff.

3, 5 *since the causes are different:* There are alternative ways of understanding this statement. Either the difference is between the soul of the cosmos (and the souls of stars and planets), that do in a sense descend, or at least enter, bodies, and the souls of individual human beings. This is how MacKenna understands it, translating (or rather paraphrasing): "Now this does not clash with the first theory (that of the impassivity of the soul as in the All (= cosmos); for the descent of the human Soul has not been due to the same causes (as that of the All-Soul)." Or else the distinction is between the different reasons for the human soul's descent—compulsion and volition. The former differences are explored in what immediately follows, the latter in chapter 5 onwards. The introductory particle at the start of the next paragraph—*toinun* (= then) marginally supports the latter; for the former we might have expected an explanatory *gar* (= for).

Lines 6–16

Plotinus now considers the way in which Intellect relates to its posteriors without engaging in the same way that souls do when embroiled in the sensible world. He is showing how Intellect can maintain its integrity even though it is undergoing some degree of pluralization and engagement with the sensible world. He is both drawing on, and disagreeing with, what Aristotle says in *Metaphysics* 12. Aristotle's first principle is Intellect, the unmoved mover, that changes / moves other things without itself being changed / moved. At 1072b8 we are told that the intellection of Intellect and the objects of its intellection are identical (cf. *de Anima* 429b23ff. where the same claim is made about perception); it is "intellection of intellection" *(noêsis noêseôs)* and is pure actuality *(energeia)*. Its cosmogonical role is to be the object of love for the heavenly bodies, which are thereby caused to move in the most perfect everlasting circular motion; this motion in the superlunary world is then transmitted to the sublunary world and is the cause of all natural change and movement. Intellect has no perception or knowledge of what lies outside itself.

So when Plotinus says that Intellect *exists whole and entire in the realm of intellection* he is accepting so far the Aristotelian concept of Intellect. But Aristotle's Intellect is more akin to Plato's and Plotinus' first principle, the Good or the One, which is unitary, transcending, and remaining entirely aloof from, its posteriors—as Plato says at *Republic* 509b "it is even beyond being, surpassing it in majesty and power"—a statement that was axiomatic for Plotinus. It is the source of the intelligible world and all that follows. For Plotinus Intellect is at one remove from the One and is already pluralized. It is, to use the terminology of Plato at *Parmenides* 144e5 "a one-and-many" *(hen-polla)*, as Plotinus does at V.4.1, 21. The primary pluralization lies in the distinction between Intellect and its objects, the Forms, whereas (as we have seen) intellection and its objects are one and the same for Aristotle. Plato expresses this through the mythological language of *Timaeus*, where the demiurge takes the place of Intellect, and contemplates the Forms as models for the organization of the cosmos through the mediation of the soul of the cosmos. Plotinus demythologizes this, as we have seen, through his doctrine of emanation. Further differentiation within Intellect is envisaged by Plotinus as the product of individual intellects.

Light may be thrown on the present passage by recourse to his doctrine of double activity as set out at V.4 [7].2 (the treatise immediately after IV.8 in Porphyry's table). For further references see Atkinson (1983, 56–57). Just as the Forms themselves are both eternal and self-sufficient but contain within themselves *logoi* (formulae, seminal reasonings) that emerge as *logoi* in their posteriors to carry forward the essential nature of the Form into the particular; in just the same way Intellect has two activities, the first contained entirely in itself and the second emerging as individual intellects to be housed in souls, as the only faculty in the case of the soul of the cosmos and the souls of the stars and planets, and as the rational faculty in human souls. See further Atkinson (1983, 51–54) for a discussion of *logoi*, where he likens Plotinus' views to those of the Stoics, who made a distinction between *logoi endiathetoi* (*logoi* in conception) inherent in the prior, and *logoi prophorikoi* (lit: "carrying forward," *logoi* in expression) in the posterior. Cf. note on 2, 32. It is important not to see clear demarcations between levels of being (hypostases), as the images of the city and the fire below suggest. See O'Meara, chapter 3 in Gerson, ed. (1996). The first or internal activity of anything is equated to its essence and called by Plotinus at V.4.2, 21 "the activity of its essence" *(energeia tês ousias)* and the second or external activity "the activity coming from its essence" *(energeia ek tês ousias)*. Plotinus' way of bridging the gap between internal and external activity is to call the internal activity a power *(dunamis)*. We need to distinguish between different senses of the word *dunamis*. He cannot be using it here it in the commoner sense of "potential," since that would allocate an inferior status to the superior partner, since activity / actuality is always superior to potentiality, at least ontologically. In any case he warns us at II.5.1, 21 to distinguish between *dunamis* (nominative case) = "power," and *dunamei* (dative case) = "in potentiality, potentially." In the case of non-reciprocal dependence, as with Form and particular, the posterior is contained potentially in its prior, but not vice-versa. See Emilsson (2007, ch. 1, sec. 1–2) for a good discussion of these points.

So in sum, in the intelligible world intellection is the first activity of Intellect; this is what constitutes Intellect and is its *power* which produces the second activity, intellection in the individual soul. As Emilsson puts it (2007, 30): "The power so described, however, is not the external act itself. It is the internal act but referred to as the productive cause of the external one."

3, 10 *there had to be many souls . . . had to be distinct:* In Plotinus' terms the whole process of emanation is a necessary one. The double activity doctrine outlined above demonstrates that at every stage of the process of emanation the hypostasis, just by being what it is, both remains self-sufficient in its essence, and at the same time by its power cannot help being the productive cause of its posteriors. In the language of *Timaeus* the demiurge, in order to impose order on otherwise chaotic matter, *has to* look at the model, the Ideal Living Creature, and *has to* work as best he can with the materials at his disposal. If the cosmos is to be perfected, then he *has to* act as he does. See Cornford (1937, 34); in this teleological view he is supported by Sedley (2007, ch. 4). Inge (1948, vol.1, 254) puts it: "All is ordered by the necessity that eternal principles should act in accordance with their own nature."

3, 11 *the one soul:* I.e., the hypostasis. Just as Intellect, in contrast to the unity of the One, is a one-and-many plurality *(hen-polla)*, so Soul (the hypostasis), at the next stage of plurality, can be called a many-and-one *(polla-hen)*. Each individual soul (the soul of the cosmos, the souls of the stars and planets, the individual human souls—the three species of generic Soul) each has intellection to a greater or lesser extent. In the case of the individual human soul we saw at 2, 43 that *the association of the soul* *with the body . . . inhibits intellection.* So too individual souls, through this association, are *better* or *worse.* For a possible distinction between *nous* in Soul the hypostasis and in individual intellects cf. *Phaedrus* 247d.

3, 14 *including everything else by its power:* Plotinus uses the dative of *dunamis* here not in the sense of "potentially" (despite what he says at II.5.1, 21. See Emilsson [2007, 30]). This use of *dunamei* can be traced back, yet again, to *Republic* 509b: "the Good is beyond being, surpassing it in power (hardly 'potential') and majesty."

3, 14 *there, in Intellect:* Plotinus frequently uses the adverb *ekei* (there) to denote the intelligible world, and *entautha* (here) to denote the sensible world.

Lines 16–20

Plotinus sets out to show that in the intelligible world, especially in the case of Intellect itself rather than the objects of its intellection, the Forms—although the same principles would apply to them—its integrity can be maintained even when it undergoes pluralization into individual intellects. He will contrast this with the case of soul at line 21.

He uses three analogies, in addition to the genus-species analogy in line 12, from the sensible world to explain the way in which generic Intellect is related to its species; despite differentiation, the essential unity of their nature is stressed.

Firstly, he draws an analogy between Intellect and *a great living creature*. The absence of the definite article suggests that he is not referring to the Ideal Living Creature but to the genus of living creature that embraces its species just as Intellect includes *everything else*—Plotinus uses a rather indeterminate neuter plural, perhaps to mean that Intellect includes both individual intellects and Forms.

Secondly, he likens Intellect to the life of a city and of its citizens (we could perhaps bear in mind the analogy between city and individual soul in *Republic*). The Greek term for "living" is *empsukhos* (lit: ensouled), a term used frequently by Plotinus to denote a living being in the sensible world—it is often, for example, linked to the word "body" *(sôma)* to indicate the living creature, otherwise often called "the conjoint," or to the word "cosmos" to denote the created universe as a living organism along the lines of *Timaeus*. Plotinus' point is that the city, as an inclusive living organism, contains many individual living organisms (the citizens), and although the former may be more complete as a living organism, even so both it and its citizens are of the same nature. The emphasis is on the ensouled nature of both city and citizens, and although the analogy pertains to the sensible world, there are echoes of the relation of Soul the hypostasis to individual souls.

Thirdly, Plotinus uses an image of which he is fond, one that recalls the double activity doctrine. For example at V.1.3, 9 he says: "In the case of fire there is one heat remaining within it and another which it dispenses" (trans. Atkinson); and at V.4.2, 22 he says: "There is an activity of its essence and the activity coming from its essence. The former is the activity which constitutes each thing, while the latter derives from it and must necessarily conform to it in every respect, although it is different from it. Just so in the case of fire there is a heat which brings its essence to completion, and another which comes into being when the fire exercises the activity which is innate to its essence in so much as it is abiding fire." The phrase *universal fire* is ambiguous. It could refer to the Form of fire, which Plotinus acknowledges, following *Timaeus* 51bff., at VI.5.8, 23. But that is unlikely, since *a great fire* and *smaller fires* stemming from it would have to refer to fires in the sensible world (possibly the elemental fire at the outer limit of the cosmos and the fires burning as stars and planets), and so would invalidate the point that Plotinus is making in this section, that the integrity of an intelligible or a sensible persists throughout its derivatives within its own frame of reference. So it refers rather to the totality of fire in the sensible world, elemental fire as described at *Timaeus* 51bff. (but that is a much disputed passage), and all sensible fires from stars down to domestic hearths. However, it may be taken more simply and refer to a physically observable conflagration and smaller fires sparked off around it; all are fire, so the fire is both one and many, just like Soul and souls (I am grateful to John Dillon for this suggestion).

However, it may be that in two of the three analogies there is a crossover between two frames of reference, from Ideal Living Creature to individual living creatures, and from the Form of fire to individual sensible fires. This crossover, perhaps originating in Plato's discussion in *Phaedo* concerning the manner of the participation of particulars in Forms, continued to exercise Platonists, a problem aired by Simplicius at *in Cat.* 219, 18. Cf. Fleet (2002, 174n305): "Latitude (*platos* lit: breadth, latitude) was a term used by the commentators (on Aristotle) to explain an apparent paradox: How can anything acquire different degrees of a quality which itself does not admit of degrees? Their answer was that the mixture of elements in a thing, through intension and remission (*epitasis* and *anesis*) in the mixture, allows a range or 'latitude' in the participation in that quality."

3, 20 *universal being:* As described above, the being *(ousia)* of each thing is its first activity—being just what it is, and is the power that produces in its posterior. This second activity in the posterior then becomes its first activity, being and power to produce its second activity in its posterior, and so on.

3, 21 *or rather the being:* Plotinus is making a distinction between the being and the activity (cf. V.4.2, 27 "an activity of [or belonging to] its being") in that the being is ontologically prior to the activity, which only emerges when the posterior turns to its prior and so gains its definition. Something comes into being as a result of emanation and so can be said to have being; but it is only subsequently that it gains its definition and becomes an activity. Or else universal fire, which is the Form or being of fire, is to be identified with being in general.

Lines 21–30

The individual soul, unlike Intellect, straddles the intelligible and the sensible worlds by its descent into bodies. Unlike the soul of the cosmos and the souls of the stars and planets it becomes embroiled and is aware of the affections of the body because it *took on something extra*, although Plotinus would always affirm the non-affectability and transcendence of the soul, and claim that an affection of the body is only an affection because it is recognized as such by the soul.

3, 2 *function:* The Greek word is *ergon*, etymologically connected with *energeia* (activity). The function of anything is what it does *qua* itself, when it is fully active. Soul turns to its prior, Intellect, and gains its definition; and in so doing receives from the activity of Intellect its own intellective activity.

3, 24 *something extra:* either (a) the lower parts of the soul, either the spirited and appetitive according to the Platonic tripartition, or the non-rational functions such as nutritional, appetitive, perceptive, generative, vegetative and impulsive (according to different Aristotelian analyses) which the demiurge ordered the lesser gods to implant, or (b) the body, or (c) both. At present we are considering *the more rational soul* but will be soon (at 4, 41) considering its acquisition of a body.

3, 25 *it looks to what is prior:* So far the soul follows the pattern of emanation; turning to its prior, gaining its definition and producing its posterior—on the cosmic scale what is produced is a sort of fourth hypostasis, often called Nature; what the individual soul produces is touched on briefly in chapter 6. The difference between Intellect and its products, and Soul and its products is that, whereas Intellect is aloof from its posteriors, Soul, as Plato tells us at *Phaedrus* 246b, "as a whole has concern for all that is unensouled," which it organizes and directs.

3, 27 *it was impossible . . . has to exist:* See above on 3, 10 *there had to be many souls.*

Chapter 4

In this chapter Plotinus begins to engage more closely with the question of descent. Individual souls, in their undescended state, share the untroubled condition of the soul of the cosmos, directing from above without effort and distress. But it is in their nature to turn not only to their prior but also to direct their "powers" to what is below them, the sensible world, in particular their own bodies. Much of the chapter is devoted to describing the increasing isolation of the human soul as it descends; there is as yet no discussion of the causes of the descent. The chapter ends with reference to *Timaeus*.

Lines 1–5

The individual soul is torn between yearning for its priors and concern for its posteriors.

4, 2 *in turning back:* The familiar turning back (or inwards) of posterior to contemplate its prior.

4, 2 *their source:* The source of soul is ultimately the One, but here the accent is on the more immediate source, Soul the hypostasis, which itself derives more immediately from Intellect, hence their *intellective yearning.*

4, 1 *a yearning which is intellective:* The Greek word for yearning is *orexis,* which in itself is no more than "a reaching out towards." But Plotinus more than once uses it in conjunction with the word for sexual love, *erôs,* e.g., at III.5.3, 23 he says: "Since there had to be a soul of this cosmos, the other love (i.e., "heavenly love") came into being along with it, itself the product of yearning"; and at III.5.1, 17: "If you were to assume that the origin (of love) was the yearning for Beauty itself already in souls . . . you would be right"; and at III.5.4, 7: "This would be the love which implants the desire according to the nature of each soul, which yearns for what is appropriate to its own nature"; and at III.5.4, 22: "Love is the activity *(energeia)* of the soul yearning for the Good." He takes his cue from Plato; at III.5.1, 6 he talks of "the divine Plato, who wrote much about love in very many places in his works; he has said that it is a kind of affection which occurs in souls that yearn [to entangle with something beautiful]." So yearning is the starting point for love. Plato talks about sexual love at many levels. He does not always condemn it in its carnal form, e.g., at *Republic* it is not to be despised as the mechanism for the production of the next generation of citizens. But it is in its philosophical form that Plotinus shows the greatest interest, perhaps with an eye to the (spurious) *Definitions* 414b: "Philosophy is the yearning for knowledge of eternal beings."

In *Republic* 403a we read: "The correct sort of love (Aphrodite rather than Eros is named) is a sober and educated love of the orderly and beautiful"; and at 490ab Plato talks about the nature of the good citizen, who must be a true lover of knowledge *(philomathês)* who will not give up his love *(erôs)* until it has had intercourse (*hapsasthai*—an equally ambiguous word in Greek and English) with the nature of each thing in itself (i.e., the Form) with the part of his soul that should lay hold of such a thing, joining in union with true Reality so as to give birth to intellect and truth, gain knowledge and truly live.

Although the sexual language in these passages could be said to be metaphorical, that is not the case in *Phaedrus*, an important text for Plotinus, in which Plato subtly weaves together different strands of erotic love. One of the main themes of the dialogue is Love, which we are told is one of the four types of divine madness, which is a gift of the gods bringing the greatest happiness (245c). In his second speech (sometimes called the Palinode) Socrates presents as the model for philosophical enlightenment the philosopher and his young male lover, and the two are seen in this part of the dialogue as a couple on a joint quest. The lover, seeing the beauty of his beloved, feels a frisson and a fever, and his wings (see Introduction, 26 for the wings in the chariot myth) begin to grow again; he feels his soul warmed and full of happiness. Eventually the love is requited by his beloved and together they enter into an orderly philosophical life: "So in this world they live a happy and harmonious life, in control of themselves and conducting themselves in a well-ordered manner."

Symposium too is a seminal work for Plotinus. Here also the topic of conversation is Love. Earlier speakers have given their eulogies, one of whom, Pausanias, says that there are two Loves, the vulgar *erôs* (who represents carnal love for women and young boys, and heavenly *erôs* (who represents "Platonic" love between an older and a younger man as portrayed in *Phaedrus*), which is lifelong and aimed at moral improvement. This distinction is echoed by Plotinus at III.5.1, 10–15.

But it is Socrates' speech in *Symposium* that Plotinus found most inspirational, and III.5 is effectively a commentary on it. Socrates tells of the instruction that he received from Diotima (see Introduction, 28ff). Briefly Love is described as an intermediary between men and gods. Love seeks for permanent possession of the good (206a); this is happiness. We are all pregnant both in body and soul. Just as we seek a beautiful woman so that we can beget beautiful children, so we seek a beautiful young man so that we can bring our spiritual offspring, wisdom and virtue, to birth, until finally the lover, now on his own, can rise to a vision and knowledge of Beauty itself (211d). See Guthrie (1975, 374–378) for a full summary of Socrates' speech. For us it is important to see how Love, in its sublime form, is the driving force behind the philosophical ascent to "assimilation with god." For both Plato and Plotinus, then, love is a single thing; carnal love is not a metaphor for philosophical love.

This erotic language was not used in the description of personal philosophical motivation by Platonists after Plato until Plotinus took it up. In Aristotle we do have Love as a motivating cosmic force, where the planets are driven by love to reproduce the motions of the Unmoved Mover, and at *EN* 1139b5 he uses the term "intellective yearning" (*orexis dianoêtikê*, but without any apparent sexual connotation. For the lack of the motif in the Middle Platonists see Thesleff (1994).

4, 2 *they also have a power:* See chapter 3, lines 6–20 on double activity for the idea that soul's activity *(energeia)* is transmitted to what is below it by its power *(dunamis)*. We are reminded of *Republic* 507b–509c, a passage that is the root of Plotinus' doctrine of emanation. Plato likens the Good in the intelligible world to the sun in the sensible world. The Good, while remaining entirely aloof, pours out truth so as to give being and intelligibility to the Forms; so in the sensible world the sun, while remaining apart from the process of *genesis* for which it is responsible, pours down its light so as to give generation, growth and nourishment. The difference with soul is that, being further on in the process of emanation, it can turn back to its prior in the way that the Good cannot (there being nothing prior to the Good), and is also aware of and concerned with its posteriors. Herein lies the root of the issue under discussion in this treatise.

Lines 5–10

Behind these lines lies the question that Plotinus grappled with throughout his life, the paradoxical nature of the soul, being both one and many, and being engaged with both the intelligible and the sensible worlds. He broaches it in some of the earlier treatises in Porphyry's table, notably IV.2 [4] and IV.9 [8], and in some later ones, notably VI.4 [22], VI.5 [23] and IV.3 [27]. Plotinus' inconsistency, as we might expect, mirrors Plato's. He is especially puzzled by *Timaeus* 41dff. where human souls are said to be made up of the same ingredients as other souls—Sameness, Difference and Being. Here in IV.8 we are told that human souls enjoy the tranquillity of the soul of the cosmos when they are performing *the function of the more rational soul* (3.21–22). There is perhaps an echo of the tranquillity enjoyed by the

Epicurean gods—the tranquillity *(ataraxia)* which is the goal of human life.

4, 5 *universal soul . . . universal soul:* The Greek expression used here is *tês holês [psukhês]*. So far, when he has talked about the soul of the cosmos he has used phrases such as "soul of the All" *(psukhê tou pantos)* using a genitive to define *psukhê*. So here, where he is using not a genitive but an adjective *(holês)* he may well be intending to refer to "soul as a whole" inclusively. If so, he is emphasizing the intelligible aspect of soul; soul in the intelligible world is undifferentiated and has taken on *nothing extra*. Thus in the analogy that follows, as far as the subjects are concerned, there is no difference between the monarch and his courtiers. There is perhaps an allusion to Plato *Letter* 2.312de where there is a cryptic announcement that "the King of all things" is the source of all things and at *Letter* 6 we are told to swear by "the god who is lord of all that is and shall be, and by the mighty father of the ruler and cause"; cf. Aristotle *DM* 398a11ff. See Loeb, Plato, vol. 9, 400 for an attempt to solve this puzzle.

Lines 10–42

In the remainder of the chapter Plotinus describes the double life of the soul in more detail. Even when it is embroiled in the sensible world it still retains a toehold in the intelligible world.

4, 10 *out of the universal:* The universal is here contrasted with the partial. Souls, while still remaining in the intelligible world *together with universal soul* (line 6) share its universality and indivisibility (i.e., they are not separated from universal soul. Cf. VI.4.8, 12ff. where Plotinus says that it is body that causes division in souls, and VI.4, 14), although there is some degree of pluralization in soul even before it becomes embroiled. The next few lines (10ff.) describe the increasing division or pluralization from being "soul as a whole" to being an *each.* Rist (1967, 127) puts it: "Their collective nature is lost."

4, 11 *belong to themselves:* MacKenna translates "they become . . . self-centred." Cf. V.1.1, 3 "The beginning of the souls' wickedness was their audacity, their birth, their first 'otherness' and the wish to belong to themselves."

4, 11 *being with something else . . . retires to its own place:* In contrast to lines 9–10 *For they are then all together in the same place.*

4, 12 *over a period of time:* In contrast to the timeless nature of the intelligible world the soul is now involved in the processes of the sensible world.

4, 13 *fleeing the All:* Flight in the direction opposite to that of *Theaetetus* 176ab: "We should try to flee from

Here to There as quickly as possible" and the last words of VI.9 "flight in solitude to the solitary."

4, 15 *grows weak:* Increasing separation from the universal is accompanied by increasing weakness. For Plotinus the weakest of all is matter, i.e., the utterly characterless nothingness that is at the very end of, even beyond, the process of emanation, the non-being of *Republic* 478d. Cf. III.6.15, 22: "Matter, being far weaker in power than the soul, has none of the real beings . . . since it is an absence of all things . . . and it cannot even say 'Here I am.'" The more embroiled in matter the soul is, the weaker it becomes.

4, 16 *it has mounted a single vehicle:* The Greek literally means "it has embarked on one single thing." This phrase was seen by later Neoplatonists (e.g., Proclus *in Tim.* 3.236, 31ff. and Philoponus *in de Anima* 18, 26–31) as proof that Plotinus believed that the human soul, after leaving its star, embarked on a vehicle that was made of breath *(pneuma)* or light *(phôs)* as an intermediary between the intelligible and sensible. Supporters of this view could look to *Phaedrus* 250c where the soul is said to be contained "like an oyster [in its shell]," the myth of the charioteer in *Phaedrus*, *Phaedo* 113d where dead souls are said to embark on "vessels *(okhêmata)* provided for them," and *Timaeus* 41e, 44e and 69c where the word *okhêma* is used to denote the container of the soul (the word is derived from the *verb ekhein* = "to have, to contain, to support" and need not have any connotations of a vehicle, although it usually does), and 44a where Plato talks of "the whole envelope *(kutos)* of the soul." For texts illustrating the long history of this "pneumatic vehicle" see Sorabji, ed. (2004, vol.1, ch. 8).

4, 17 *turned:* Turned in the wrong direction, to what is outside itself, away from itself and its priors.

4, 18 *battered on all sides: Timaeus* 43a and 69cd talk of the violence done to the human soul on its entry into the sensible world.

4, 19 *with great difficulty:* The Greek phrase is *meta peristaseôs*, translated by Armstrong as "with great difficulty" and by the medieval Arabic *Dicta Sapientis Graeci* ("Sayings of the Sage," i.e., Plotinus) as "with toil and fatigue," but by MacKenna as "by an actual presence." The word itself is initially neutral in meaning = circumstances, but takes on secondary meanings, especially to denote critical circumstances.

4, 20 *through contact . . . being present:* These phrases emphasize the increasing involvement of the soul in the body. One of the most formidable problems for a Platonist—especially in the face of Aristotle's criticisms—was to explain, or even describe, the relationship between soul and body (cf. Porphyry *VP* 13.10). Soul is of a higher order than body and is what produces body, with which it enters "an uneasy partnership" (IV.4.18, 33). We are here dealing not with unensouled *(apsukhos)* body, but with ensouled *(empsukhos)* body, "body of such-and-such a kind" *(sôma to toionde)* to use an Aristotelian term. We need to demythologize *Timaeus* and see the presence of soul in body not as an arrival, but as a permanent state. Cf. Wilberding (2006, 171): "Body is a necessary product of soul (V.8.12, 17) and as IV.3.13, 12–14 suggests, even soul's organization *(dioikêsis)* of a living thing involves soul's producing body." It is thus paradoxical that the soul is ensnared by the very thing it has produced.

4, 21 *sinking deep inside it:* A reversal of the state Plotinus describes at 1, 1–3 *I often wake up from my body into my true self, so that being within myself and outside all other things I enjoy a vision of wonderful beauty.* Instead of withdrawing into his true self, he sinks deeper into the sensible world.

4, 22 *moulting . . . fetters:* See note on chapter 1, lines 23–50 and Introduction, 25ff. on *Phaedrus.* Cf. *Phaedrus* 250c, where Plato is talking of the state of philosophical enlightenment in which ". . . we are not entombed in what we now carry around and call the body, being imprisoned after the fashion of an oyster."

4, 23 *invulnerability:* The Greek word is *ablabês*, an adjective that can have either an active ("doing no harm") or a passive ("suffering no harm") force. Plotinus uses the same phrase at II.1.4, 32 "the direction of the cosmos does the soul no harm and causes it no trouble." Armstrong takes it in the former sense "it has missed the immunity which it had," but MacKenna in the latter "the soul has lost that innocency of conducting the higher."

4, 25 *had soared back upwards:* The Greek verb is made up of the prefix *ana-* which can mean either "up" or "back," and the verb proper *trekhô* which means "to run" or "to hasten." So there is perhaps a double sense—the soul soars upwards on its newly regrown wings, but is also returning home to where it belongs.

4, 26 *entombed in a cave:* See note on chapter 1, lines 23–50, and Introduction, 21–24.

4, 30 *recollection:* The immediate reference is to *Phaedrus* 249e: "As stated, every human soul has by nature seen the true realities; otherwise it would not have come to this living creature. But it is not easy for every soul to gain *recollection* of things There from things Here." Plato's most extensive presentation of his doctrine of Recollection is at *Phaedo* 72eff. and *Meno* 81aff., where he demonstrates that prior to incarnation the soul has knowledge of the Forms, which it loses at the moment of birth and subsequently attempts to regain—more or less successfully depending on progress made in philosophy *(those more able to consort with Intellect).* Plotinus has little to say about the doctrine apart from this mention and a more extended passage at V.3.2. See Blumenthal (1971, 96–97) and Gerson (1994, 179–180), neither of whom take this passage into account. Blumenthal suggests that Plotinus rejected the doctrine in favor of his claim that the higher part of the soul remains always in the intelligible world, as instanced in chapter 8 of this treatise. But the generally cursory treatment given by Plotinus does not mean that (at least at this stage of his life) he did reject the doctrine. This is suggested by the subsequent words *to live one life There and one Here, turn and turn about.* However, the Greek phrase *para meros* could mean not "turn and turn about" but "in division, partially" and be applied just to the life Here, as opposed to the life There which is single, undivided.

4, 30 *it always keeps something in some way transcendent:* The Greek word for "transcendent" is *huperekhôn*, the word Plato assigns to the Good at *Republic* 509b where he says "it is even beyond being, surpassing (= transcending) it in majesty and power." The *something* is some knowledge of the Forms, even if temporarily "forgotten."

4, 34 *by nature or chance:* Plotinus is accounting for the moral and intellectual differences between individuals.

Nature could have one of two meanings here. Either he could mean "nature" in the sense of the quasi hypostasis, the product of the "power" of soul, the sensible world. If so it should be taken closely with "chance" as a single concept, the chance occurrences in nature. As we have seen, the demiurge in *Timaeus* is working on pre-existing chaotic matter, which can never be totally subdued by reason, and it is these forces that do violence to the descending soul from every side in a chance and random way. Each soul responds differently to these forces. Or else he is making a distinction between such outer forces and the inner nature of the human individual; we all start off the same at our first incarnation, but great discrepancies occur when we come to choose our second and subsequent lives, as Plato describes, for example, in the Myth of Er in *Republic* 10, which is preceded in *Republic* 8 by a description of different types of character; he also hints at it in *Timaeus* 42b. At 42c he uses the same word "nature" *(phusis)* in conjunction with the adjective bestial *(thêreion)* to denote the bestial nature that an individual might sink to after a series of wicked lives. The only redemption comes when the circles of the Same and the Different in the soul regain their equilibrium. Plotinus bears this out at III.2.13, 11ff. where he states that our present lives are to an extent determined by our past lives: "A man does not become a slave or a prisoner of war, nor is his body abused at random; he was once the perpetrator of what he is now suffering." He acknowledges different natures at III.4.6, 8–10: "The soul does not always act correctly, since it is of such a disposition that it is of such-and-such a kind in such-and-such a particular condition and so has a particular life and makes particular choices."

4, 36 *the second mixing bowl:* This refers to *Timaeus* 41d, where the demiurge is making up the individual souls from the same ingredients as he had made the soul of the cosmos (see note on 2, 35 *what is in its nature*), but these are no longer quite as pure as formerly. In fact the demiurge uses the same bowl for a second time, not a second bowl. He then divides the contents up into parts, each part being an individual soul. As with the soul of the cosmos, the blends of Being, Sameness and Difference allow for individual souls to engage both ontologically and epistemologically with both the intelligible and the sensible worlds. This is what he means by the clause *since they had become parts of a particular kind;* now that they were divided up as individuals they had to proceed to the necessary division among bodies. *Dicta Sapientis Graeci* paraphrases: "Plato said that when the creator divided the souls out of the last goblet and made them like the particular things, he made them descend of necessity to *genesis*, since they had become particular, suited to *genesis*."

4, 37 *they had to enter: Timaeus* 41e, where the demiurge explains the laws of Fate and the appointed incarnation.

There is considerable emphasis on necessity in this passage of *Timaeus.*

4, 38 *And if he says:* The reference to *sowed* is to *Timaeus*, e.g 41c, 42a and 42d, where the demiurge sows the rational parts of individual souls.

4, 39 *he has him talk:* The demiurge addresses his children, the lesser gods, at *Timaeus* 41a–d, instructing them to weave the mortal and immortal together to create the other kinds of living creatures—terrestrial, winged, aquatic.

Plotinus is defending Plato's mythologizing, which is *to make his exposition clear.* Some Platonists, notably Atticus and Plutarch, understood *Timaeus* to be describing a process that took place in time. This is a position that Plotinus rejects unequivocally, seeing *Timaeus* as a myth that expressed a state that is non-temporal, eternally subsisting. He expresses his views most forcefully at III.7.6, 50ff.: "When Plato says 'it was good' he is referring us to the concept of the All, indicating that by the term 'the transcendent All' it had no beginning in time; so not even the cosmos had a beginning in time." See Sorabji (1983, ch. 17) for a discussion of the literal and non-literal interpretations of *Timaeus*, and Sedley (2007, 95–107).

4, 40 *things which exist in the nature of universals* is a puzzling phrase. MacKenna translates "what is rooted in the nature of the All," and Armstrong: "the things which exist in the nature of the Whole." Both translate the plural *tôn holôn* as singular, which does not square with Plotinus' normal usage, where the plural tends to indicate "wholes" as opposed to "parts." The demiurge certainly does not create Forms, which are described at 51e as "unchanging, ungenerated, imperishable." So what Plotinus is talking about here must be things in the sensible world which in the narrative of *Timaeus* are created in time by the demiurge or the lesser gods, such as the genera of living creatures, but which in reality are everlasting. Perhaps the best fit is "genera" as opposed to individuals. Thus when he goes on to talk about things *which are everlastingly coming into being in this way and which are everlastingly existing* he is not making the typical distinction between transient particulars and eternal archetypes, but using the term *existing* merely to indicate existence in the sensible world. The word *everlastingly* is used not to denote some eternal intelligible, but merely the fact that the sensible world, although full of transitory inhabitants, is itself everlasting. Alternatively he may have in mind Aristotle *Metaphysics* 7 1038b1ff., where Aristotle explores (and rejects) the possibility that substance may be the universal on the grounds that it is more knowable than the particular (cf. *Posterior Analytics*

8b6ff.) and that it endures while the particulars do not. Bréhier on the other hand sees this as an allusion to *Timaeus* 37d, where the demiurge creates time as "the moving image of eternity" and translates "Plato envisages things that are in the nature of the cosmos to be engendered and created, and believes that they display in their sequence eternal events and realities."

Chapter 5

PLOTINUS NOW BEGINS to address the reasons for the descent of the human soul into the sensible world. He is at pains to show that the doctrines of Plato form a coherent whole, and that there are no real discrepancies between necessity and volition. He warns us of the perils and punishments that beset the soul that becomes too embroiled, but reminds us that this is not the lot of every human soul; it is possible for us both to engage with the sensible world and to retain our integrity. There is a teleological emphasis throughout the chapter, and it is by an understanding of the teleology that we can reconcile the apparent paradox. This teleological framework has already been introduced at 1, 41–48. In *Timaeus*, as the demiurge proceeds with the creation of the cosmos, Plato prefaces the details with a strong teleological statement at 29d: "Let us, then, state for what reason becoming and this universe were framed by him who framed them. He was good; and in the good no jealousy in any matter can ever arise. So, being without jealousy, he desired that all things should come as near as possible to being like himself. That this is the supremely valid principle of becoming and of the order of the world, we shall most surely be right to accept from men of understanding. Desiring, then, that all things should be good and, so far as might be, nothing imperfect, the god took over all that is visible—not at rest, but in discordant and unordered motion—and brought it from disorder into order, since he judged that order was in every way the better" (trans. Cornford). This principle is reiterated at 41a–d in the demiurge's address to his children, the lesser gods: "If mortal creatures are not born, the heavens will be imperfect. For it will not contain all the kinds of living being, as it must, if it is to be perfect and complete." Similarly the construction of the human body and the implanting in it of the soul (as described at 69aff.) are directed to the same end. So the overall purpose of the demiurge in creating the cosmos is to embody the Ideal Living Creature, and all his efforts and the efforts of the lesser gods are directed to the fulfillment of that purpose. A necessary part of the scheme is the creation of the souls of individual humans (and by extension of all living creatures) whose perfection is to be achieved by assimilation to god. But it would not be enough just to create souls already assimilated—that would be to create a static cosmos (as Sedley suggests, like building a zoo but putting no animals in it) and would not instantiate the Ideal Living Creature, but be more like the sterile One Being of Parmenides. The part played by the descent and ascent of the human soul is eloquently summarized by Inge (1948, 254): "They were created and sent into the world that they might be moulded a little nearer to the Divine image by yearning for the home which they have left." The cosmos is the theater of operations in which the human soul is to find perfection, and this can be found only through the application of its own volition. In the cosmos, however, it is subject to "violent impressions, desire, pleasure, pain, fear, anger and all variety of affections" (42ab).

The question arises whether these turbulent conditions are caused by the inherently unruly character of the contents of the Receptacle, which the demiurge never quite completely subdues or whether he has completely mastered them (the recurring phrase "as well as possible" is ambiguous) and is exploiting their characteristics to allow human souls the scope for the philosophical and moral development that will lead to assimilation. For an excellent discussion of this point see Sedley (2007, ch. 4, sec. 1–5). Whatever the case, that is not an issue at play in this treatise, where the question is rather: Given that the cosmos is a dangerous place—for whatever reasons—why should the human soul plunge into it?

Plotinus has already told us at 1, 23ff. that there are many apparent inconsistencies in Plato's thinking; here in chapter 5 he attempts to find consistency. At lines 7–8 *(nor, generally speaking, is there a discrepancy between the voluntary and the involuntary nature of the descent)* he identifies what is at the root of the apparent inconsistency.

First, some of Plato's texts suggest that the descent is involuntary. Of these the most significant is *Timaeus*, which, as we have seen above, makes the descent a necessary act on the part of the demiurge in perfecting the sensible copy of the Ideal Living Creature. The other important text in this respect is *Republic* 519c–520d; the philosopher-king must be compelled to return to the Cave, however reluctant he or she is, "by persuasion or compulsion."

Secondly, by contrast *Phaedrus* shows us that the soul is self-moving: "Every body whose source of movement is outside itself is unensouled; but whatever has the source of motion within itself is ensouled, since this is the nature of soul" (245d–246a). In the ensuing myth at 246dff., the soul is likened to a charioteer and his two horses; sometimes the willfulness of one of the horses drags the whole chariot down to earth; "There is commotion, competition and a great amount of sweating, where, through the incompetence of the charioteers many souls are lamed or have their wings damaged." In this case Plato is ascribing the descent—the loss of wings, the moulting—to the wrongly directed self-movement in the soul. There is no element of compulsion.

Thirdly, there are passages where both the involuntary and the voluntary are found side by side, or rather one after the other. In the Myth of Er in *Republic* 10, in the myth at the end of *Gorgias*, in *Phaedo* 81d–82b, and in the continuation of the *Phaedrus* myth souls are compelled to choose their next life or else (in *Phaedo*) to enter it without choice, or to draw lots *(Phaedrus).* But within this framework there is also room for the voluntary. Souls are judged on the quality of their previous life and are held responsible for the good and bad in it. Although there is always in the background the Socratic maxim "no-one willingly does wrong" (*Laws* 731c and 860d), nevertheless the praise or blame apportioned by the judges pre-supposes at least a degree of moral responsibility. Then, in the Myth of Er, souls are given the choice of their next life, and although the choices might seem predictable Plato does not suggest that they are pre-determined. Presumably the choices between different courses of action go on during the lifetime. Although the vocabulary and the concepts of choice and free will are different from our own, there can be no doubt that Plato was not an out-and-out determinist. See Leroux in Gerson, ed. (1996, ch. 12) for a discussion of these terms.

These, then, are the strands in Plato's thought that Plotinus is seeking to interweave.

Lines 1–8

Plotinus begins by listing the Platonic phrases that might seem to imply inconsistency, together with phrases from Empedocles and Heraclitus. I have put inverted commas round them in the translation, although they are not necessarily direct quotations. These lines are largely a recapitulation of what Plotinus has already said, and I list them here with their occurrences earlier in the treatise (see notes *ad loc.* for references to Plato, Empedocles and Heraclitus).

sowing seed for birth	4, 38
the descent for the perfection of the world	1, 48–50; 2, 20
judgment	1, 38
the cave	1, 33; 3, 4–5; 4, 28
necessity	1, 40
volition	2, 5
being in the body which is something evil	1, 29–30; 1, 40; 2, 42–45; 3, 1–3
flight from god	1, 19
the sin which brings judgment	1, 18
repose consisting in flight	1, 14

5, 3 *for necessity includes volition:* These two are not polar opposites, mutually exclusive, but volition is included within the framework of the necessity of birth and rebirth as outlined above. This is to put the involuntary and the voluntary in parallel; we have to descend to fulfill the purpose of the demiurge, and in so doing we find we actually want to. The Stoics too, especially Chrysippus, attempted to include choice within the framework of necessity; see LS section 62.

See Leroux in Gerson, ed. (1996, 296–297) for a good discussion of this concept; he makes a distinction between the freedom of the soul to ascend and its "pre-empirical" freedom to descend; a good summary is *Dicta Sapientis Graeci* 5: "All these statements (i.e., the ones quoted by Plotinus at the start of this chapter) come down to one meaning: the descent into this world occurs both willingly and unwillingly. Willingly, because of the soul herself, for she desired to be with her actions; unwillingly because she was sent by the first cause, her creator and originator."

5, 5 *Empedocles' wandering:* This is fragment 115 = KRS 401. "The oracle of necessity decrees that the soul who is guilty of the sins of bloodshed and perjury will *wander* for 30,000 years apart from the blessed, going through successive incarnations . . . I myself am one such, a wanderer and exile from god" like those (fragment 118 = KRS 402) "who *wander* in darkness over the meadow of doom."

Lines 8–16

Plotinus shows that there is a (teleological) purpose in the descent of the soul, however involuntary.

5, 8 *For everything that goes to the worse:* It was a commonplace of Greek philosophy that everything seeks what is best for it; e.g., the start of Aristotle's *Nicomachean Ethics:* "Every science and every investigation, similarly every action and every choice, seems to aim at some good; so it has been rightly declared that the good is 'that which everything aims at'"; cf. *Gorgias* 468c and *Philebus* 20d. Plotinus goes on to point out that if something (he keeps to the general neuter "it" rather than the feminine "she" = "the soul" right down to line 16) goes to the worse by its own momentum, then blame is to be attached to it.

5, 8 *by its innate momentum:* This is an ambiguous phrase. The Greek word for *momentum* is *phora*, which is generally used of imparted motion from the passive sense of the verb *pheresthai* "to be carried" and its cognates. But the adjective *innate (oikeia)* suggests that this is not an imparted motion. (Mackenna translates "inherent tendency.") Plotinus is talking about animate beings, as the phrase *experiencing justice for what it has done* indicates. *Phora* can apply to either "upward" motion to its prior, or "downward" motion to its posteriors; the latter is the motion in question here.

5, 10 *to act and be acted upon:* The contrast has been established in the previous sentence with the words *suffering* (= being acted upon) and *has done.* When applied to the human soul *to act* refers to the voluntary nature of the descent, and *to be acted upon* to its involuntary nature; the demiurge orders it *by the law of nature.*

5, 12 *it encounters:* The soul's first encounter in its descent is the body (described at 3, 26 as *what is posterior to it, [which it] organizes, and directs*) which it is to ensoul, to create the conjoint of the soul and body. This is the function of soul (*Phaedrus* 246b "soul as a whole cares for everything that is unensouled") and applies equally to individual human souls and the soul of the cosmos, although in the latter case it cannot be said to be *going to the worse.*

5, 14 *for even if:* The absolute starting point *(arkhê)* of everything is the One, but in this context we are clearly meant to see the demiurge as the starting of the necessary train of events whose course we see traced from line 10. But there is an implied contrast with lines 8–10, especially the phrase *its innate momentum.* In the case of the human soul its affections can be traced back to the compulsion applied by the *law of nature,* and to its own volition—the *self-willed inclination* of line 26.

Lines 16–24

Plotinus abandons the generalizing neuter and returns to the feminine to bring the argument back to the soul, and examines more closely the voluntary aspect of the soul's descent. Souls divide broadly into two categories; those of philosophers and morally good people, who suffer no long-lasting harm by their sojourn in the body, and those who become embroiled in the sensible world to their detriment. Both suffer some sort of *penalty* or requital. It might seem harsh to classify the former as falling into *error* (some translations prefer the language of sinning) when they have been compelled to descend and apparently do little or nothing wrong. Therein lies the paradox. They are compelled to descend, but it is in their nature to agree to the compulsion, whereby it acquires a voluntary component. Emanation means that they engender their posteriors. If souls did not have the yearning to turn downwards to their posteriors, they would not have the yearning to turn back again on the upward path to assimilation. We need to sin before we can find redemption. The behavior of the soul in its descent and embroilment in its own posteriors is vividly described at V.1.1: "Whatever is it, then, that has caused souls to forget God their father, and although sharing in that world and belonging completely to him to be ignorant both of themselves and of him? The beginning of their wickedness was their audacity, their birth, the first 'otherness' and the wish to belong to themselves. When they had appeared in this world, they took pleasure in their free will *(autexousion)* and made much use of their self-movement," trans. Atkinson; Rist (1967, 121–122) points to a passage at IV.3.13, 17 where the voluntary nature of the descent is likened to a sexual urge.

5, 19 *just what it has suffered after descending:* The price paid by the souls of the righteous is to be exposed to the psychic and bodily affections that *batter* it from all sides, from which they can *escape quickly* (*Timaeus* 42ab). The price paid in the latter case can consist in further incarnations, described by Plato at *Republic* 619b–e, *Phaedrus* 248de and 249b, *Timaeus* 42b; these accounts, couched as myth, vary a little; in some the souls of the righteous escape rebirth altogether, in others only after a number of rebirths. But in more extreme cases the souls of the wicked are despatched to places of torment, as in *Phaedrus* 249a, *Phaedo* 81de, *Gorgias* 523ab, and *Republic* 615b and 616a.

Lines 24–37

Plotinus now turns his attention briefly to considering the human souls whose *error* is less, concluding with a statement affirming the necessity of descent.

5, 24 *the soul is something divine:* As Armstrong (Loeb, vol. 1, 132n) notes: "Soul is of course a god for Plotinus, though of the lowest rank." For Plotinus the most compelling evidence comes from Plato. The human soul is made of the same ingredients as the soul of the cosmos. The cosmos itself is described at *Timaeus* 34a and 34b as a god; and at 34c the soul of the cosmos is said to be earlier and prior to the cosmos in "birth and excellence." So *a fortiori* the soul of the cosmos is divine, and so then is the human soul as being made of the same mixture of ingredients. It is no surprise that a god can be created—the demiurge creates the lesser gods, and at 40b assigns them to the stars that are themselves "divine and everlasting beings." Plotinus commonly uses the term "divine" to denote the intelligible world.

5, 24 *comes from the higher realm:* As being the second activity of Intellect it straddles the intelligible and the sensible worlds, and thereby shares some of the divinity of the intelligible world.

5, 26 *through self-willed inclination: Self-willed (autexousios)* is a word frequently used by Plotinus, without a pejorative sense, to indicate freedom of will, e.g., 3.4.4, 37: "Creatures that have self-willed movement in themselves may sometimes incline to what is better, sometimes to what is worse." Both in that passage and here he also uses the term *inclination*, as does Plato in *Phaedrus* 247b to denote the downward pull exerted by the unruly horse on the rest of the chariot team. The two words together give a strong indication of freedom of choice, and underline the voluntary aspect of the soul's descent.

5, 28 *acquiring a knowledge of evil:* Philosophy will give us a knowledge of (good and) evil, and set us on the road to assimilation, as in the curriculum of the philosopher-kings in *Republic*. Plotinus' view of evil is monistic. The One, paradoxically, is the ultimate source of evil, which he here tells us is part of the necessary experience of the incarnate human soul. This monistic approach is fundamental to Plotinus' thinking, and his concept of evil is closely bound up with his concept of matter; but again the testimony of Plato is not entirely clear or consistent. In *Timaeus* the demiurge sets himself the task of imposing order on an otherwise unruly disorder according to a pattern *(paradeigma)*. One view, the traditional view, is that he does not entirely succeed in reproducing the perfection of the pattern owing to the imperfection of his material, and that this imperfection is the cause of evil in the generated cosmos, including the souls of humans. This view is persuasively challenged by Sedley (2007, ch. 4, sec. 5) on the grounds that the demiurge, as a master craftsman, would not use the materials (and he uses all the materials) at his disposal in any way other than so as to produce a perfect creation. "Would Plato's theology," Sedley says (2007, 116), "really allow that the best thing in the universe, god, might on occasion be defeated by the lowliest thing, matter?"

However, Plato nowhere fully discusses the question of evil. Guthrie (1978, vol. 5, 92–100) reviews the question and its treatment by scholars, who are divided on the consistency of Plato's approach; some consider that he moved away from a monistic position, in which evil is seen as the absence of good, to a dualism where there is a positive evil force at work in the world. (See further Cherniss [1971, 244–258].) Plotinus affirms the monistic approach in many places, especially in the anti-Gnostic treatise II.9. I.8 is devoted to a discussion of evil; chapter 3 establishes the concept of absolute evil, and chapter 5 identifies this evil with matter, and it is further defined in chapter 7, where Plotinus begins by stating that evil is the necessary antithesis of good: "But why is it necessary for evil to exist if good does? Is it because matter must exist in the universe? Yes, because the universe is of necessity made up of contraries, and would not exist if matter did not exist." This is supported by *Timaeus* 47e5–48a1, and *Theaetetus* 176a6: "There must always be an opposite to good." Plotinus describes matter as the end of the procession from the Good at I.8.7, 17ff.: "Since the Good is not the only thing that exists, it is necessary that, by the procession from it, the Last should exist—after which nothing else can come into being—and this is evil. What is after the First is of necessity, so that the Last too is of necessity. This is matter, which has nothing of the Good in it; and this is the necessity of evil." Matter is utter deficiency, what is left when all qualities have been stripped away, and as the antithesis of Good it is—by being utter deficiency of Good—itself utter evil. Inge (1948, vol. 1, 131) makes a distinction between this evil which is to do with existence (and is part of the very fabric of being) and a secondary evil which is to do with value—existential as opposed to moral evil. Soul's involvement with matter is an essential part of its time in the sensible world and is a necessary feature of the teleology. Moral evil—the error—in the soul derives from its inability to see the material aspect of the sensible world for what it is. But the existential evil in the cosmos is not an error (or the product of a failing on the part of the demiurge), and so not amenable to blame and punishment; it is a fact of existence and part of the grand teleological design. Blame is to be apportioned only to the soul that allows itself to be seduced and contaminated by the material world. But an understanding of it is a necessary part of assimilation; hence Plotinus states: *If it escapes quickly it will have suffered no damage by acquiring a knowledge of evil, by having learnt about the nature of vice.* Perhaps the *evil* is the existential evil, and *vice* the moral evil.[23]

5, 29 *bringing its powers into the open:* Individual souls cooperate with the soul of the cosmos in bringing the cosmos into being, or rather sustaining its being.

23 Much of this note is drawn from Fleet (1995, 206–208).

The cosmos, modelled on the Ideal Living Creature, is thereby itself a living creature, every part of which is pervaded by soul (*Timaeus* 34b: the demiurge puts soul at the center of the cosmos and wraps it around the outside); the soul of the cosmos is what brings the otherwise unensouled to life. Individual souls mirror this process on a microcosmic scale in the case of individual bodies, pervading and enlivening them at every level, from the rational to the merely vegetative, throughout a lifetime. Descent into bodies describes as events in time, in the terms of the myth of *Timaeus*, what in Plotinus' view was an everlasting process. The engagement of soul with body is constant and progressive during the lifetime of a person as he or she grows up and becomes not only physically mature but also, more importantly, morally mature. Part of this engagement is the ability to make choices of our own volition. Correct choices lead to assimilation; wrong ones to increasing alienation.

So to fulfill the teleological purpose the process of emanation must progress. The human soul plays its part by *bringing its powers into the open and by displaying its functions and actions.* If the process of emanation were to be stifled (which is in fact impossible) then the perfection of the cosmos would not be achieved and the human soul would not gain its redemption.

5, 35 *Each one of us:* The chapter ends on an optimistic note, probably in contrast to the Gnostic view that the cosmos is an evil creation. Part of our human experience is the ability, through philosophy, to gain a vision of the beauty of the intelligible world by contemplating the beauties of the sensible world.

Summary of Chapter 5

If we step away from the metaphorical language of ascent and descent, and look behind the mythology of cave, prison and punishment, what do we learn of Plotinus' views on the human condition? The cosmos is a purposeful whole under the direction of a benign god; each one of us is a member of this cosmos. And beyond this visible and material cosmos of the here and now there is a higher intelligible world to which we aspire. As a conjoint of soul and body I cannot help being alive; I did not choose to be born; I am here perforce—although before my rebirth I do have some choice about my next life. My soul is inseparable from my body during my lifetime, which it enforms to create the living me. But I did have choice; I can choose to remove soul from body—but suicide is distasteful for most, and certainly for Plotinus, as he points out in the very brief treatise I.9. So I willingly live my life in the body; that is punishment enough. But I can choose to remove soul from body in a different sense through a life of philosophy and achieve, albeit momentarily during my lifetime, assimilation; and so I can live a morally virtuous life, turning my back on the material and sensual. All this is "up to me"; I can and must make choices. Many of us make wrong choices and give way to the temptations of the world and the flesh; then the punishment is severe.

Chapter 6

IN THIS CHAPTER Plotinus pulls together threads from earlier chapters, addressing in particular the necessity that pervades the whole process of emanation, from its starting point in the One to its completion in matter. This is the framework within which are to be seen the activities of soul. We should bear in mind that Plotinus, like Plato in *Timaeus*, uses the language of an unfolding narrative as a tool of analysis to describe an eternally continuing state of affairs, "*to make his exposition clear.*"

Lines 1–6

In these lines Plotinus reminds us that a single structure includes both the intelligible and the sensible worlds, and that any generation of the cosmos comes about by necessity. For this he would need to look no further than *Timaeus* 29d: "So let us state the reason why the author of the world of becoming and the cosmos created them. He was good, and no jealousy can occur in one who is good, at any time over anything. So being free of jealousy he wanted everything to be as like himself as possible." Plotinus follows the metaphysics of being that Plato outlines in *Republic* 6 in the image of the Divided Line, which presents a spectrum from the Good "which is beyond being" at the one extreme, to the shadowy world of images that stands just above non-being at the other. What lies between includes both the intelligible and the sensible worlds, the latter being an image of the former; it may be illusory, but is not an illusion—it has "being of a sort"—something rejected by Parmenides, who denied the plurality of becoming and posited just the sort of *static* and (counter-intuitively) unchanging One Being to which Plotinus alludes in line 3. (For Parmenides see KRS, Graham [2006], Warren [2007], and Mourelatos [2008].) In these six lines we are shown the three levels within the intelligible world.

(a) *unity;* the One that is the origin of *all things*
(b) *real beings;* Intellect and its objects, the Forms, which themselves would be *lacking shape* and would not *exist* if they did not turn back to the One to gain definition
(c) *the beings that came after them;* souls; Intellect and the Forms *(the plurality of those beings)* could not help "overflowing to produce Soul"—although

> Plotinus here includes all souls that, as we know from 5, 24, are *something divine and come from the higher realms.* It is only by "overflowing" that Intellect and the Forms fulfill their nature and so complete their definition (see Gerson [1994, 22–41]).

Both the One and Intellect remain aloof from their posteriors—line 10 tells us *what is prior remains for ever in its proper abode*—unlike soul, as we shall see.

6, 2 *shape:* The Greek word is *morphê* which is often used to denote Form; but the regular word for Form is *eidos*, which Plotinus avoids here, since to say the Forms would be formless would be clumsy.

6, 5 *issued:* Plotinus' word is *proödos*, a noun that he frequently uses to denote the "procession" outwards from the One.

Lines 6–18

Plotinus now considers the nature of emanation in the sensible world. The principle is the same; soul, by its nature, produces posteriors. But in this case the product is the cosmos. In the case of the soul of the cosmos the product is the whole of the cosmos (the All, as Plotinus sometimes calls it) which we have learnt at 2, 14 *is perfect, fully adequate and self-sufficient, and contains nothing contrary to its nature.* The individual human soul, by contrast, as we have seen especially in chapter 5, does not remain aloof; it descends.

6, 8 *as from a seed:* Armstrong (Loeb, vol. 4, 414) compares III.7.11, 23–27, where it is rather the soul as "seed" that initiates the process of generation, with less happy results.

6, 11 *some ineffable power:* See notes on *powers* at 3, 6–21. The power in the soul that engenders its posteriors accords with the power that pervades the intelligible and sensible worlds alike, and brings all things to *the ultimate limit of their potential*, i.e., the completion or perfection of the sensible world. Plotinus stresses in these lines the seamless nature of the whole of being. The same power reaches down from the One to the end of the process of emanation, so that all things *have a share in the nature of the good.*

6, 13 *jealously:* An echo of *Timaeus* 29d, quoted above.

The emphasis in lines 13–18 *(until all things . . . to participate)*, with the repetition of *all things . . . anything . . . each thing*, is on the power of the One that pervades the entirety of the intelligible and sensible worlds. The question remains whether *matter* is to be included, and it is to *matter* that Plotinus now turns his attention.

Lines 18–28

In what follows I draw largely on Fleet (1995, 164–167).

Plotinus offers alternative explanations of the origin of matter:

(a) line 18 *If . . . the nature of matter has always existed*
(b) lines 20–21 *if the coming to be of matter was a necessary consequence of prior causes.*

But he does not overtly commit himself to either, but only to the conclusion that matter does in some sense participate. His dilemma has its roots, once again, in a lack of clear direction on the part of Plato. Plotinus tends to use Aristotelian terminology when discussing matter, such as *hulê* (matter) and *to hupokeimenon* (the substrate). Despite Aristotle's remarks at *Physics* 4.2 209b11, Plato does not use the word *hulê* in a technical Aristotelian sense. But Aristotle's words there and at 210a 1–2, despite their apparent carelessness, suggest that the Receptacle of *Timaeus* was being equated to *hulê* at a very early stage, possibly within the Academy itself, as do Theophrastus' words (fr. 48 Wimmer): "He [Plato] wants to make two principles, the one being the substrate in the form of matter, which he describes as all-receptive, and the other as cause and moving agent, which he attaches to the power of God and of the Good." Theophrastus was Aristotle's successor as head of the Lyceum, and possibly a pupil of Plato, so these remarks come early on in the post-Platonic era. Sandbach (1985) gives references to passages in later Platonists (Plutarch, Alcinous, Aetius) to show that they too accepted the identification. What is more significant is the idea of matter in the "pure" sense that Plotinus defends became fused with the idea of matter as a material substrate to corporeal bodies. The problem can be traced back to *Timaeus*. In giving his account of the generation of the cosmos Plato adds to the two factors already identified by 48e (the model and the copy of the model) a "third kind" *(triton genos)* which he designates variously as "the Receptacle of all becoming . . . like a nurse," "the nature which receives all bodies," "that in which" and "the [kind] always consisting in space." It is entirely without qualities, and any descriptions of it are negative, e.g., "allowing no destruction," "it does not depart in any way from its own character," "it is apprehensible by none of the senses," "it has never in any way at all taken any shape *(morphê)* similar to what has entered it" and "it is beyond all the Forms." However, there are some passages in *Timaeus* where Plato's language suggests a rather more plastic nature for the Receptacle. We are told that "it is the base in which all things are moulded, moved and shaped by what enters." We are given four analogies for the Receptacle. Gill (1987, 34–53) explains these as follows: that of the nurse (49a6 and 52d5) illustrates the receptivity and capacity to nurture, that of the gold (50a6) its permanence, that of the soft material

(50e8) its characterlessness, and that of the winnowing basket (52e6) its function as space. It is only the last of these—the only one that occurs after the identification of the Receptacle with space *(khôra)*—which does not suggest some idea of matter as a material substrate. I would add Plato's mention of the traces *(ikhnê)* of the elements already present in the Receptacle before the demiurge gets to work. From all this there developed a quite different concept of matter as the material substrate common to schools such as the Stoics and Peripatetics. Thus there are two separate accounts of matter current soon after the writing of *Timaeus*, both of which can be traced back to the dialogue. First there is the "purist" account to which Plotinus subscribes, and secondly the "non-purist" account that seems to have become commonly accepted. In the process of synthesization matter had lost the entirely negative character of Plato's Receptacle, a nature that Plotinus was anxious to reaffirm.

Plotinus further identifies matter with non-being. O'Brien in Gerson, ed. (1996, ch. 7, sec. 1) suggests that when Plotinus describes matter in this way, e.g., at III.6.7, 1, he is thinking of *Sophist* esp. 237bff. O'Brien summarizes: "When Plotinus says that matter is 'non-being' he does not mean that matter does not exist . . . but that non-being (but not 'non-being in and by itself' [= what is not in any way at all] is an essential condition of the existence of any object, since all objects, except only being itself, participate in otherness in relation to being, and in so far as they are 'other than being' must therefore be counted as 'non-being.'"

For Aristotle substances can be analyzed into Form and matter at different levels. For example at one level a house is Form (the overall design) imposed on matter (the bricks, beams, etc.); at the next level down a beam of timber is similarly a case of Form (its shape, purpose) imposed on the matter (timber); and so on down to the basic four elements. What is not clear is whether Aristotle posited some sort of matter that could not be further analyzed in this way, "bare matter" underlying even the four elements—perhaps because that ceases to be a scientific issue and enters the realms of metaphysics. See Charlton (1970, 129–145) and Gill (1989, 243–252).

[It should be noted that Plotinus is not here concerned with intelligible matter *(hulê noêtê)* which acts as the substrate in the intelligible world to the One who generates Intellect and the Forms; for this Plotinus draws on the One and the Indefinite Dyad of *Philebus*.]

So Plotinus does subscribe to the concept of bare matter, but with the qualification that it can *participate*. O'Brien's remarks noted above are much to the point. This is a good example of Plotinus interpreting Plato through the lens of Aristotle, but an Aristotle carefully refined to suit his argument.

The two options offered at 18–21 are, then, that matter has existed eternally depending for its being, such as it is, on the munificence of the One, or that it is in some way generated by *prior causes*, the implication being that this generation took place in time. If the distinction is between a non-fundamentalist and a fundamentalist reading of *Timaeus*, then Plotinus would not accept the second alternative. Rist (1967, 117–119) points to the phrase *not even in this case* as signalling Plotinus' rejection of the notion. But what the *prior causes* might be is not clear. What Plotinus could not countenance is some other creator such as the evil demiurge of the Gnostics. It is possible that by *prior causes* he means some other proximate causes, such as soul, mediating between the One and the cosmos within the overall causative role of the One, or the lesser gods who are charged by the demiurge with the creation of the lower parts of the human soul and their bodies (*Timaeus* 42dff.), or even the pre-existing elements in the Receptacle (though it would make little sense to call these causes of themselves). Brehier (1958, 180) suggests that the distinction is between matter as independent of the process of emanation and matter as the end point of emanation, a view rejected by Rist. Whatever the correct interpretation of this difficult passage, Plotinus' conclusion is clear:

matter is more than "non-being in and by itself"; it has an essential role in the being of the cosmos. As such Plotinus can use the term at line 18 *the nature of matter*, and allow that matter can participate.

Lines 23–28

The last few lines of the chapter, 23ff. *(So the very great beauty . . .)* remind us

(a) of the unity of being, from the One to matter,
(b) that it is the product of a good demiurge.

Let Sedley have the last word (2007, 122): "The presence of moral badness and unhappiness in individuals is not a mark of the world's imperfections, provided that those defects play a necessary part in the bigger picture of cosmic justice."

Chapter 7

IN THIS CHAPTER Plotinus further explores the nature of the soul by comparing and contrasting the activities of Intellect, individual soul and the soul of the cosmos.

Lines 1–5

The human soul lies partway between the intelligible and the sensible worlds, and should be content with its situation.

7, 1 *this nature:* The twofold nature is that of the soul, part to do with the intelligible world, part to do with the sensible world, reiterated in line 3: *since it has the sort of nature that it has.* Alternatively the twofold nature may be that of the intelligible and sensible worlds themselves; *sensible nature* is a phrase used in line 7. This is an echo of the phrase at *Timaeus* 42a: "Since human nature is twofold"; but there the division is not the same, but between man and woman.

7, 2 *it is better for the soul to have its being in the intelligible world:* the closer to the One (= the Good) the better.

7, 2 *it must of necessity have the ability:* It is necessary if the design of the demiurge is to be perfected, a conditional necessity that is applied to the entire work of the demiurge, although the necessity of emanation is not conditional. *Necessity (anagkê)* and its cognates are words used repeatedly at *Timaeus* 42a and 69cd. Archer-Hind notes *(ad loc.)* that in 69c "*necessarily*" means "inherent in their [souls'] nature," i.e., non-conditional necessity.

7, 3 *participate:* The word commonly used by Plato and Plotinus to denote the relation of particulars to Forms; particulars "participate" or "share" in Forms (cf. 6, 15 [of the One] *it . . . cannot leave anything without a share in itself*). Here the order is reversed, and soul is said to participate in its posteriors.

7, 4 *in that it is not superior in all respects:* The Greek is ambiguous. Armstrong translates: "Granted that all things are not the best." Either interpretation makes good sense. The soul might feel aggrieved because it is of lower rank to its priors, or because it is assigned to an inferior station. Cf. III.3.3, 9–19.

Lines 6–17

Plotinus reaffirms the teleological view that the soul must experience evil in order to know good.

7, 6 *it belongs to the divine realm:* The vocabulary is reminiscent of chapter 1, line 3. *Divine* is an adjective frequently applied by Plotinus to the intelligible world, especially to Intellect, e.g., "assimilation to the divine." Cf. 5, 24 *although the soul is something divine and comes from the higher realm* and *Phaedrus* 230a where Socrates claims "to belong by his nature to a divine . . . realm."

7, 7 *and borders on:* Cf. IV.4.3, 11: "[Soul] lives on the borders *(methorion)* and as such it is turned in two directions," and 4, 32: "Souls come to have two lives *(amphibioi)* . . . one There . . . one Here." Cf. Trouillard (1949, 355); he suggests that the real self oscillates between the upper and lower limits of soul "*in a sort of multivalency . . . this pluralism with its internal conflicts is essential to the human condition.*"

7, 8 *to receive something from it:* What it receives from the sensible world is initially harmful. We have seen throughout this treatise what some of the harmful effects are for the soul from its association with body. Plato too warns us at *Phaedo* 64d–65a of over-attention to the demands of the body, and at *Republic* 611e the soul is said to be defiled by its association with the body and other evils. But ultimately good can come of it too; we can gain a knowledge of evil and vice (5.28), and this is a necessary part of the soul's salvation. Cf. 5, 36 *For now, each one of us, seeing the outer richness, marvels at the inner reality and the creation of such subtleties.*

7, 9 *if ever it should not organize:* This is in contrast to 2, 23 *for it is no way an evil for the soul to give body the power of well-being and existence.*

7, 9 *the secure part of itself:* The Greek word for *secure* is *asphalês*, which literally means "not tripping up," so perhaps we have an echo of "the error of the soul" discussed in 5, 16ff. *The secure part* is the rational faculty; if, like the charioteer himself in the myth in *Phaedrus*, this remains in full control of the other, lower, faculties, then no harm can come to the soul.

7, 10 *sink into the interior:* The verb "sink" is used at 2, 46; 4, 21 and 5, 19–20, in contrast to the vocabulary of "ascent."

7, 10 *excessive eagerness:* This refers to the process described in chapters 4 and 5, especially the *self-willed inclination* at 5, 26. The soul must, by its nature, engage with the body, but it can be overenthusiastic and, like Narcissus, fall in love with its own image.

7, 10 *not remaining whole along with the whole:* The increasing pluralization described at 4, 10: *the individual souls move out of the universal to become partial.*

7, 12 *having gained some record:* The Greek word for *record* is *historia*, which (as its English derivative suggests) implies learning by inquiry. Here the soul profits by the knowledge it has gained.

7, 13 *By comparing what are in a way opposites:* Since the point Plotinus is making is that experience in the sensible world can lead to an understanding of the contents of the intelligible world *(the nobler things)* he cannot be talking about good and bad as opposite qualities instantiated in particulars in the sensible world. Rather he is suggesting that experience of evil in the sensible world can lead us to an understanding of the Form of Good in the intelligible world. So they are only opposites *in a way*. In any case evil is not a Form; at I.8.1, 12ff., where Plotinus denies that evil can be Form and says that it is not an opposite so much as a privation, he says: "But if—since knowledge in the case of opposites is one and the same, and since evil is the opposite of good, and since knowledge of good will also be knowledge of evil—then those who intend to know what evil is must have a clear perception of good, since the better is prior to the worse and a Form, while the worse is rather a privation." There is an interplay in lines 13–17 between understanding and experience, a twist on the saying "to suffer is to learn." At root is the fundamental Platonic distinction between knowledge or understanding, whose theater is the intelligible world, and experience or suffering, whose theater is the sensible world. Hence Plotinus continues to be guarded in his use of language; the soul *in a way* understands the contents of the intelligible world, as opposed, for example, to the would-be philosopher-kings in *Republic* who gain *real understanding* only at the end of their studies.

7, 15 *for those whose powers are too weak:* Either those who are weak by nature, or those who have become weakened by association with the body as at 4, 15. Plotinus seems to be excluding those souls guilty of the first error described at 5, 16ff., although they too *suffer after descending.* He is rather concerned with both groups of those guilty of the second error.

The Arabic *Theologia* paraphrases: "For if the knower is weak by nature and has experience of evil and knows it by experience, that is one of the things that increase him in the knowledge of good, by learning and demonstration, this being better than that he should know evil by knowledge only, not by experience." But this seems to ignore the force of the repeated *in a way*.

Lines 17–22

Plotinus sets up a comparison between Intellect and soul, beginning with Intellect.

7, 17 *the outward progress of Intellect:* In these lines Plotinus is concerned with the overflowing of Intellect in the process of emanation rather than with its turning back; the subject of the verbs *(it . . . it . . . it . . . it)* is *outward progress*, not *Intellect* (although the final *it itself rises swiftly back upwards* does seem to refer to Intellect). At III.8.9, 31 Plotinus describes Intellect as "facing in both directions" (*amphistomos*, which is reminiscent of *souls come to have two lives [amphibioi]* at 4, 32); he goes on to say that it cannot see the One without ceasing to be entirely Intellect. He then proceeds, using the term "outward progress" *(diexodos)* six times, to describe the outflowing of Intellect to its posteriors. So in this part of the chapter Plotinus is showing that Intellect overflows, but only so far, *to the limit of what is inferior* (MacKenna: "a descent to its own downward ultimate"). It is not clear what he means by the phrase *the limit of what is inferior*. Is it the upper limit of Soul, or the lower limit of Intellect—although in a way these are one and the same? The meaning seems to be that that Intellect cannot itself become Soul—which is the overflow of Intellect turning back to its prior to gain definition—without departing from its nature. It is its nature to overflow, to make an *outward progress*, and in so doing to create the raw material for the next stage, Soul. Then it can *rise swiftly back upwards*, not to the One (that has just been specifically ruled out) but to itself. We are given a dynamic picture of sequential movement down and up, out and in, although there in truth no sequence of events but rather a continuous oscillation.

Lines 23–32

Plotinus now turns his attention to soul, and compares and contrasts the activity of the individual soul with that of the soul of the cosmos. He starts with a general statement that what is above soul is its priors, the contents of the intelligible world, and what is below it is the cosmos and its contents (lines 23–24). In the case of the individual soul *(souls that are in division and in an inferior position)* contemplation of its priors is constrained by *time;* it happens during the lifetime of the individual human. The soul of the cosmos, by contrast, is *for ever depending on its priors*. It does not *become involved in this inferior activity* (embroilment in the sensible world) so it has no suffering or *experience of evils*. But it must by its nature *touch upon this world*, since "all soul cares for the unensouled";—like the detached rule of the monarch at 4, 7. The cosmos at large is perfect and needs no interference, but only a directing hand (2, 16 *it requires only a brief word of command*). The character of its engagement is *intellectively . . . in contemplation.*

7, 28 *embraces intellectively:* The Greek term is *perinoein;* cf. VI.9.11, 24, where the contemplation of the godhead in his sanctuary by the seer is said to be "a reach towards contact . . . a meditation *(perinoêsis)* towards adjustment" (trans. MacKenna). Soul, both individual and the soul of the cosmos, being products of Intellect, have intellective capacities; but as we have seen at 2, 43 *the association of the soul with the body . . . inhibits intellection.*

7, 30 *minister:* The Greek verb is *khorêgein*, used at 6, 20 *matter . . . participates in that which bestows (khorêgountos) the good on everything*, and at 4, 5 to indicate generosity.

Chapter 8

PLOTINUS ENDS THE TREATISE on an optimistic note. Whatever difficulties the soul experiences in the body, there is always a part of it that does not descend but remains in the intelligible world. This is the *true self*. It is always available to us, even when the lower soul is *mastered and thrown into turmoil*. Return to it constitutes assimilation to the divine.[24]

Lines 1–6

Plotinus tells us that he is affirming this belief *against the opinions of others*. There is no record of its appearance among the Middle Platonists, and it appears to be an innovation on the part of Plotinus, so these *others* must refer to his contemporaries either within or outside his circle, although they remain unnamed. Nor did it receive

[24] For an interesting comparison of Plotinus' views with those of Aristotle see M. F. Burnyeat: *Aristotle's Divine Intellect*, Marquette University Press, Milwaukee, 2008.

much support after Plotinus' time. Simplicius (*in Cat.* 191, 8–12) tells us that Iamblichus followed Plotinus in this belief, but that statement has received some modification. R. M. van den Berg has shown that Iamblichus thinks that a few perfect souls have the unextended status that Plotinus attributes to all of us (see *Syllecta Classica* VIII: *Iamblichus: The Philosopher*), and Proclus (*in Tim.* 3 333, 28ff.) adds Theodorus. For the continuing debate after Plotinus' time on this topic see Sorabji, ed. (2004, vol. 1, 93ff).

Plotinus reiterates the doctrine in treatises written, according to Porphyry's order, at various times in his life. IV.3 [27].12, 1–3 tells us that the souls of men are not cut off from their principle *(arkhê)* and Intellect, and "even though they have descended, yet their higher part holds for ever above the heavens" (trans. MacKenna); II.9 [33].2, 5 tells us that "one part of our soul is always directed to the world There"; and VI.7 [38].5, 26 that "the diviner part of the soul does not depart from the intelligible world, but is joined with it, while the lower soul hangs down from it." And at V.1 [10].10, 13ff. he gives his reasons: "This reasoning part of the soul, then, which needs no bodily organ for its reasoning, but keeps its activity pure so that it may also reason purely, is separate and unmixed with body; if you were to set it in the intelligible world, you would not be wrong. We must not look for a place in which to position it, but it must be put outside all place; for the expressions 'by itself,', 'outside' and 'immaterial' apply to it only when it is alone, possessing nothing from the nature of body" (trans. Atkinson).

There is no overt statement of the doctrine in Plato, and there are places where it would seem to be ruled out. In the charioteer myth in *Phaedrus* it is the whole soul that plunges to earth—charioteer and the two horses. The education of the philosopher-kings in *Republic* and the ascent from the cave give no hint of dormant upper soul. The doctrine of Recollection in *Phaedo* and *Meno* gives no clues either.

But Plotinus could find adequate material in *Timaeus:*

(a) the demiurge reserves for himself the immortal rational part of the soul, giving it a privileged status;
(b) it is of the same mixture as the soul of the cosmos, so that it could be said to operate in the same manner; the Circle of the Same represents Reason (36c and 40a) in the soul of the cosmos, showing ceaseless and intelligent life (36e).

So if the rational part of the individual soul is modelled on the soul of the cosmos, then it too could be said to share its properties.

Another model that Plotinus could well have had in mind is to be found in Aristotle *de Anima* 3.4–5. In chapter 4 Aristotle identifies as intellect the part or faculty of the soul by which it knows *(ginôskei)* and thinks *(noei)*. In chapter 5 he divides intellect into active and passive intellect, and he characterises the former as an intellect which makes all things, is separable, impassive, unmixed, is in activity by its essence, is immortal and eternal; nor does it think intermittently. What is more, it stands to its objects as sense-perception does to its. All these characteristics are shared by Plotinus' undescended soul.

Lines 6–13

In these lines Plotinus stresses the unity of soul to avoid the criticism that if there are different parts of the soul, then each part may have its own faculties such as memory and imagination (discussed at IV.3.25ff.), and fail to communicate throughout the soul. This difficulty is already foreshadowed in, e.g., *Phaedrus;* do the three parts of the soul, as represented by the charioteer and his team, each have three faculties of soul (rational, spirited and appetitive)? And does each of these have three faculties, and so *ad infinitum?* The same problem can be seen in the different classes in the city in *Republic;* presumably the common people have more than just appetites.

These lines address the question by showing how the intellectual activity of the higher soul is shared by the other parts.

8, 6 *for the object of intellection:* The Greek term is *to noêthen*, lit: that which has been thought. This is not quite the same as the Form, since Plotinus seems to be making a distinction between the non-discursive nature of pure intellection *(nous)* whose object is the Form, and the discursive reasoning (*dianoia* or *logismos*) whose objects are of a more complex and propositional nature—the distinction made at 1, 8. This is transmitted down by the reasoning faculty to a sort of clearing house described here as *our inner powers of perception or of discursive thought.* This power can work in the opposite direction and receive occurrences in the appetitive part of the soul. Just what these *inner powers* are is not clear. Armstrong suggests "the discursive rather than the intuitive part," and *Theologia* "the cogitative and intellective faculty." The meaning seems to be that noetic experiences, consisting either in assimilation or in merely grasping the Form remain unperceived until transmitted to the rest of the soul discursively through this middle part. It is perhaps unhelpful to seek the traditional tripartite division of the soul here, but rather to think of it as a continuous whole—"one nature with many powers" as Plotinus puts it at II.9.2, 6.

Lines 13–23

In the concluding few lines Plotinus contrasts the activities of the soul of the cosmos with those of the individual soul, and ends by reaffirming that all soul is drawn together at the upper limit.

8, 13 *The soul which is whole:* This is the soul of the cosmos. It is *whole* in that it does not have different parts or faculties in the way that individual souls do to match the different functions, but only in the sense of orientation, up and down.

8, 14 *effortlessly:* Reminiscent of Xenophanes fr. 25 (KRS, 171): "God shakes everything by intellect without effort," and Aeschylus *Supplices* 100: "All the gods' work is effortless."

8, 14 *transcending . . . transcendent:* At *Republic* 509b the Good "transcends even Being."

8, 15 *art does not deliberate:* This a quotation from Aristotle *Physics* 2: "Yet art does not deliberate; if ship design were inherent in the timber, it would act in just the same way as nature." Plotinus' meaning is that the soul of the cosmos does not deliberate, since deliberation implies discursive thought which implies pluralization. It directs the cosmos by (non-discursive) intellection. Cf. VI.7.1ff.

8, 16 *organizing what is below it:* Editors suspect that there is some textual corruption; Armstrong leaves these few words untranslated. But there is clearly a contrast between the cosmic operations of the soul of the cosmos and the partial operations of the individual soul; *they belong to a part* in that they belong to a part of the whole.

Lines 17–22

These lines outline the dangers and difficulties that beset the soul on its arrival in the body.

8, 17 *they too contain the transcendent:* All souls have a common principle *(arkhê)*.

8, 20 *lacking:* Whereas the cosmos lacks nothing (*Timaeus* 33c).

8, 21 *alien . . . pleasures:* The vocabulary is reminiscent of *Phaedo* 114e; the good man rejects *pleasures* as being *alien* to him.

8, 23 *this part lives a life of consistency:* A cryptic ending; the undescended part of the soul lives a life of consistent contemplation, of constant assimilation to the divine.

Select Bibliography

Texts and Translations

Armstrong, A. H. *Plotinus.* Greek Text with English Translation and Introductions. Cambridge MA: Loeb, 1966–82.

Bréhier, E. *Plotin Ennéades.* (7 vols.) Greek Text and French Translation with Introductions and Notes. Paris, 1924–38.

Harder, R., Beutler, R., and Theiler, W. *Plotin.* (12 vols.) Greek Text with German Translation and Commentary. Hamburg 1956–71.

Henry, P. and Schwyzer, H.-R. *Plotini Opera* I-III (editio maior). Bruxelles, 1951–73. (HS_1)

Henry, P. and Schwyzer, H.-R. *Plotini Opera* I-III (editio minor, with revised text), Oxford, 1964-82. (HS_2)

MacKenna, S. *Plotinus. The Enneads.* English Translation Revised by B.S. Page. London, 1962[3].

MacKenna, S. *Plotinus. The Enneads.* Selected Treatises Revised with Notes by John M. Dillon. London: Penguin, 1991.

Arabic Commentaries

Lewis, Geoffrey. English Translations of Sections of Two Medieval Arabic Commentaries on the *Enneads* (1. *Theologia Aristotelis* ["The Theology of Aristotle"], dating from the 8th century, 2. *Dicta Sapientis Graeci* ["Sayings of the Greek Sage"], dating from the 10th century; the "Greek Sage" is not named in the commentary, but is certainly Plotinus. These give useful insights into Plotinus' thought), in Henry, P. and Schwyzer, H.-R. *Plotini Opera* Vol. II (HS_1).

Lexicons

Lexicon Plotinianum. J. Sleeman & R. Pollet. Leiden: 1980.

A Greek-English Lexicon. H. Liddell & R. Scott, 9th ed. revised by H. Jones. Oxford: 1940.

General

Archer-Hind, R. D. *The Timaeus of Plato.* London: Macmillan, 1888.

Armstrong, A. H., ed. *The Cambridge History of Later Greek and Early Medieval Philosophy.* Cambridge: Cambridge University Press, 1970.

Atkinson, Michael. *Plotinus. Ennead* V.1: *On the Three Principal Hypostases*. Oxford: Oxford University Press, 1983. Reprinted with corrections, 1985.

Barnes, J. *The Presocratic Philosophers*. London: Routledge, 1982.

Benson, Hugh H., ed. *A Companion to Plato*. Oxford: Blackwell Publishing, 2006.

Blumenthal, H. J. "Soul, World Soul and Individual Soul in Plotinus." Le Néoplatonisme; colloques internationaux. Paris: CNRS, 1971.

Bréhier, Emile. *The Philosophy of Plotinus*. Translated by J. Thomas. Chicago: Chicago University Press, 1958.

Burnet, John. *Plato's* Phaedo. Oxford: Clarendon Press, 1911.

Burnyeat, Myles. *Aristotle's Divine Intellect*. The Aquinas Lecture. Milwaukee: Marquette University Press, 2008.

Charlton, W. *Aristotle's Physics* 1 & 2. Oxford: Oxford University Press, 1970.

Cherniss, H. *The Riddle of the Early Academy*. Berkeley: University of California Press, 1945.

Cornford, F. M. *Plato's Cosmology*. London: Routledge, 1937. Reprinted, Indianapolis, Hackett, 1997.

Dillon, John. *Alcinous: The Handbook of Platonism*. Oxford: Clarendon Press, 1993. Reprinted, 1995.

———. *The Middle Platonists.* London: Duckworth, 1977. New edition, 1996.

Dodds, E. R. *Pagan and Christian in an Age of Anxiety.* Cambridge: Cambridge University Press, 1965. New edition, 1991.

———. *Plato:* Gorgias. Oxford: Clarendon Press, 1959. 2nd revised edition, 1990.

Dufour, R. *Plotin sur le Ciel.* Paris: Libraire Philosophique J. Vrin, 2003.

Emilsson, E. K. *Plotinus on Intellect.* Oxford: Clarendon Press, 2007.

Ferrari, G. R. F. *Listening to the Cicadas: A Study of Plato's* Phaedrus. Cambridge: Cambridge University Press, 1987.

———., ed. *The Cambridge Companion to Plato's* Republic. Cambridge: Cambridge University Press, 2007.

Fine, Gail, ed. *Plato 2: Ethics, Politics, Religion and the Soul.* (Oxford: Oxford University Press, 1999.

———, ed. *The Oxford Handbook of Plato.* Oxford: Oxford University Press, 2008.

Finamore, John F., and Dillon, John M. *Iamblichus'* De Anima. *Text, Translation, and Commentary.* Leiden: Brill, 2002.

Fleet, Barrie. *Plotinus. Ennead* III.6: *On the Impassivity of the Bodiless.* Oxford: Clarendon Press, 1995.

———. *Simplicius on Aristotle's Categories* 7 & 8 London/Ithaca, NY: Duckworth/Cornell University Press, 2002.

———. *Simplicius on Aristotle's Physics* 2. London/Ithaca, NY: Duckworth/Cornell University Press, 1997.

Gerson Lloyd, P. *Plotinus*. London & New York: Routledge, 1994.

———., ed. *The Cambridge Companion to Plotinus*. Cambridge: Cambridge University Press, 1996.

———., ed. *The Cambridge History of Philosophy in Late Antiquity*, (2 vols) Cambridge: Cambridge University Press, 2010.

Gill, Mary Louise. *Aristotle on Substance: The Paradox of Unity*. Princeton: Princeton University Press, 1989.

Graham, Daniel W. *Explaining the Cosmos: The Ionian Tradition of Scientific Philosophy*. Princeton: Princeton University Press, 2006.

Guthrie, W. K. C. *A History of Greek Philosophy*. Vols. 4 & 5. Cambridge: Cambridge University Press, 1975 & 1978.

Hackforth, R. *Plato's* Phaedrus. Cambridge: Cambridge University Press, 1952. Reprinted, 2001.

Henry, P. *Les Etats du Texte du Plotin*. Etudes Plotiniennes 1. Paris/Louvain, 1961.

Inge, W. R. *The Philosophy of Plotinus.* 3rd edition, 2 vols. London/New York/Toronto: Longmans, Green, 1948.

Kahn, Charles H. *The Art and Thought of Heraclitus.* Cambridge: Cambridge University Press, 1979.

Kraut, Richard, ed. *The Cambridge Companion to Plato.* Cambridge: Cambridge University Press, 1992.

Lloyd, G. E. R. *Aristotle: The Growth and Structure of his Thought.* Cambridge: Cambridge University Press, 1968.

Mourelatos, Alexander P. D. *The Route of Parmenides: A Study of Word, Image, and Argument in the Fragments.* New Haven: Yale University Press, 1970. Revised and Expanded Edition. Las Vegas: Parmenides Publishing, 2008.

O'Brien, D. "Le Volontaire et la nécessité: Réflexions sur la descente de l'âme dans le philosophie de Plotin." Revue Philosophique, 167 (1977), 401–422.

O'Meara, Dominic J. *Plotinus: An Introduction to the* Enneads. Oxford: Oxford University Press, 1993.

Rist, J. M. *Plotinus: The Road to Reality.* Cambridge: Cambridge University Press, 1967.

Rowe, Christopher. *Plato:* Symposium. London: Aris & Phillips, 1998.

Sandbach, F. H. *Aristotle and the Stoics*. Proceedings of the Cambridge Philological Society, Supplementary vol. 10. Cambridge: Cambridge Philological Society, 1985.

Sedley, David. *Creatonism and its Critics in Antiquity*. Berkeley: University of California Press, 2004.

———. "The Idea of Godlikeness." In *Plato 2: Ethics, Politics, Religion, and the Soul, edited by Gail Fine*, chapter 14. Oxford: Oxford University Press, 2000.

———. *The Midwife of Platonism*. Oxford: Clarendon Press, 2004.

Sorabji, Richard. *The Philosophy of the Commentators. Volume 1: Psychology*. London: Duckworth, 2004.

Stamatellos, Giannis. *Plotinus and the Presocratics*. New York: SUNY Press, 2007.

Taylor, Thomas. *Select Works of Plotinus*. London: 1895.

Thesleff, Holger. *The Pythagorean Texts of the Hellenistic Period*. Åbo, Finland: Åbo Akademi, 1965.

———. "Notes on Eros in Middle Platonism." Arctos 28 (1994), 115–128.

———. "Notes on Unio Mystica in Plotinus." Arctos 14 1980), 101–114.

Trouillard, J. *La Liberté: Actes de IVème Congrès de philosophie de langue francaise*. Neuchâtel, 1949.

Warren, James. *Presocratics: Natural Philosophers before Socrates*. Durham, UK: Acumen Publishing, 2007.

Wilberding, J. *Plotinus' Cosmology: A Study of* Ennead *II.1 (40): Text, Translation, and Commentary*. New York: Oxford University Press, 2006.

Witt, R. *Albinus and the History of Middle Platonism*. Cambridge: Cambridge University Press, 1937.

Index of Ancient Authors

Index of Names and Subjects

• ALSO AVAILABLE FROM PARMENIDES PUBLISHING •

PRE-SOCRATICS

By Being, It Is: *The Thesis of Parmenides* by Néstor-Luis Cordero
To Think Like God: *Pythagoras and Parmenides. The Origins of Philosophy.* Scholarly and fully annotated edition by Arnold Hermann
The Illustrated To Think Like God: *Pythagoras and Parmenides. The Origins of Philosophy by* Arnold Hermann with over 200 full color illustrations.
The Legacy of Parmenides: *Eleatic Monism and Later Presocratic Thought* by Patricia Curd
Parmenides and the History of Dialectic: *Three Essays* by Scott Austin
Parmenides, Venerable and Awesome: *Proceedings of the International Symposium* edited by Néstor-Luis Cordero
The Route of Parmenides: *Revised and Expanded Edition, With a New Introduction, Three Supplemental Essays, and an Essay by Gregory Vlastos* by Alexander P. D. Mourelatos
The Fragments of Parmenides*: A Critical Text with Introduction and Translation, the Ancient Testimonia and a Commentary* by A. H. Coxon. Revised and Expanded Edition edited with new Translations by Richard McKirahan and a new Preface by Malcolm Schofield

PLATO

God and Forms in Plato by Richard D. Mohr
***Image and Paradigm in Plato's* Sophist** by David Ambuel
Interpreting Plato's Dialogues by J. Angelo Corlett
One Book, the Whole Universe: *Plato's* Timaeus *Today* edited by Richard D. Mohr and Barbara M. Sattler
***The Philosopher in Plato's* Statesman** by Mitchell Miller
Platonic Patterns: *A Collection of Studies* by Holger Thesleff
Plato's Late Ontology*: A Riddle Resolved* by Kenneth M. Sayre
***Plato's* Parmenides:** *Text, Translation & Introductory Essay* by Arnold Hermann. Translation in collaboration with Sylvana Chrysakopoulou with a Foreword by Douglas Hedley
Plato's Universe by Gregory Vlastos
***A Stranger's Knowledge: Statesmanship, Philosophy, and Law in Plato's* Statesman** by Xavier Márquez

ARISTOTLE

***One and Many in Aristotle's* Metaphysics**—*Volume I: Books Alpha-Delta* by Edward C. Halper

***One and Many in Aristotle's* Metaphysics**—*Volume 2: The Central Books* by Edward C. Halper

Reading Aristotle:* Physics *VII.3 "What is Alteration?" *Proceedings of the International ESAP-HYELE Conference* edited by Stefano Maso, Carlo Natali, and Gerhard Seel

HELLENISTIC PHILOSOPHY

A Life Worthy of the Gods: *The Materialist Psychology of Epicurus* by David Konstan

THE ENNEADS *OF PLOTINUS*
—WITH PHILOSOPHICAL COMMENTARIES
Series edited by John M. Dillon and Andrew Smith

Plotinus,* Ennead *IV.8: On the Descent of the Soul into Bodies. Translation with an Introduction & Commentary by Barrie Fleet

ETHICS

Sentience and Sensibility: *A Conversation about Moral Philosophy* by Matthew R. Silliman

AUDIOBOOKS

The Iliad (unabridged) by Stanley Lombardo
The Odyssey (unabridged) by Stanley Lombardo
The Essential Homer by Stanley Lombardo
The Essential Iliad by Stanley Lombardo

FORTHCOMING

Presocratics and Plato: *A Festschrift in Honor of Charles Kahn* edited by Arnold Hermann, Vassilis Karasmanis and Richard Patterson

Plotinus,* Ennead *V.5: That the Intelligibles are not outside the Intellectual-Principle; and on the Good. Translation with an Introduction & Commentary by Lloyd Gerson

Plotinus,* Ennead *IV.7: On the Immortality of the Soul. Translation with an Introduction & Commentary by Barrie Fleet

Aristotle's Empiricism: *Experience and Mechanics in the Fourth Century BCE* by Jean De Groot